ESCAPE

TO CLAUDIA & GORDON

George Fuller

ESCAPE

AGAINST ALL ODDS
A SURVIVOR'S STORY

George Lubow

iUniverse, Inc.
New York Lincoln Shanghai

ESCAPE
AGAINST ALL ODDS A SURVIVOR'S STORY

iUniverse, Inc.

For information address:
iUniverse, Inc.
2021 Pine Lake Road, Suite 100
Lincoln, NE 68512
www.iuniverse.com

ISBN: 0-595-32973-X

Printed in the United States of America

THIS BOOK IS DEDICATED IN MEMORY OF

My Grandmother **LEA LUBCZANSKI** killed December 8, 1941
My Mother **Beilke OSTASZYNSKI-LUBOW** killed August 7, 1942
My Brother **Osher OSTASZYNSKI-LUBOW** killed May 7, 1943
My Uncle **Yankiel LUBCZANSKI**—killed December 8, 1941
My Aunt **Chana LUBCZANSKI**—killed December 8, 1941
My cousins **Gitel and Celia LUBCZANSKI** killed December 8, 1941
All killed in Nowogrodek by the German Nazis and their collaborators

My Grandfather **Zvi Hirsh LUBCZANSKI** Died in Nowogrodek 1940
My Father **Beines OSTASZYNSKI-LUBOW** Died in the USA 1975

Jan JARMOLOWICZ
Josefa JARMOLOWICZ
Magdalena CIMOSZKO
RIGHTEOUS GENTILES WHO'S NAMES ARE NOW ENSHRINED
AT **"YAD VASHEM"**
IN JERUSALEM

**THE LAST REQUEST OF THE HOLOCAUST VICTIMS WAS TO
REMEMBER THEM AND TO TELL THEIR STORY**

Contents

Acknowledgements

For typing Peggy Hardaker. For proof reading my daughter Elana. For editing Jim Walters and Rabbi J.B. Sacks. Picture layout by Pearl and Vance Tyree

FOREWORD

My name is George Lubow, I was born in 1925 in a small town *(shtetl)* of Nowogrodek in what was once eastern Poland, now Byelorussia. The city had a population of 12,000, 50% Jewish. I came to the United States in 1949. I'm a survivor of the holocaust.

While many of you have heard of the death camps, like Auschwitz, Dachau or Buchenwald—it is important to remember that there was another method by which the Nazis killed hundreds of thousands of Jews.

Behind the advancing German army came a military group called *"ein-satzgruppen"*. The sole purpose of this Nazi military group was to march from village to village in the pale of Poland and Russia, and systematically kill the Jews. The German called it *"aktionen"*, actions. We called it slaughters or, in plain Yiddish *"shechita"*.

I witnessed and survived the first mass slaughter of December 8, 1941—when all able-bodied Jews of my home town Nowogrodek were ordered to assemble in a few city buildings, in what was once the regional Polish court complex.

Here I witnessed the selection: who should live and who should die.

The scenes I witnessed will stay with me the rest of my life. For the few survivors it will be remembered as the first of four mass slaughters in our home town. In one day over 5,000 Jews were slaughtered. They were buried in an open ravine in the forest of *"scridleve"* only three kilometers from the city.

About 1,000 Jews survived. The survivors were placed into a ghetto, only to be killed at a later date.

I survived two more slaughters one on August 7, 1942 and the second on January 4, 1943. When the number of Jews dwindled to a few hundred we were put into an *"arbeits lager"* labor camp. I was sure that if I stayed in the labor camp, I would be killed. To survive I had to escape from the camp.

On a cold wintry day on February 18, 1943 my brother Paul and I with the help of my father and my brother Osher—managed to escape from the camp. We made our way to a friendly polish farmer in the village of "Kuscino" where we were hidden in an underground bunker. What we hoped would be a short stay in the underground bunker lasted 18 long months. Just like Ann Frank, whose diary many of you have read, we faced the possibility of being discovered. We had many close calls, but because of the underground bunker we managed to avoid detection. I'm not going to dwell on the hunger and discomfort we endured. At the end 8 of us, 7 men and 1 woman survived We were liberated by the Russian army in July 1944.

The name of the farmer was Jan Jarmolowicz, his wife Josefa Jarmolowicz and their lifelong maid Magdalena Cimoszko. Righteous gentiles who's names are now enshrined at *"Yad Vashem" in Jerusalem*. My brother and I made arrangements in 1995 for the granddaughter of Jan and Josefa Jarmolowicz to be present in Israel, to accept a medal and proper recognition for her grandparents righteous deeds. The medal for Magdalena, since she had no family was placed in the museum of Tel-Aviv.

My generation of survivors is passing on. It will be the duty of the second and third generation to remember and tell our story. There are people in the world today who would like to change history, who claim that the Holocaust never happened. I write these words down to tell my story first hand.

1

GEORGE LUBOW—EARLY YEARS

The atmosphere of Europe was tinged with war as early as 1936 my tenth year. It was at this age that I first became aware of the political situation in Europe as I read the headlines in the Polish daily newspapers in bold red type on the Civil War in Spain.

The Spanish Civil War had little effect on our daily lives, yet an undercurrent of apprehension concerning the aftermath of the Civil War affected us.

It was the first time in my life that cities were bombed and civilians were killed. Little did I know that this war was only a testing ground for the horrors to come.

Against this background, my father wrote to our relatives in the United States about the possibility of our immigrating to America. The letter was plain and simple; my father inquired about the requirements for the seven of us to leave Poland for the States. The answer was prompt and to the point. In order for us to come to the United States, our relatives would have to put up a guarantee, supported by cash in the bank totaling $35,000 ($5,000 per person), that none of us would become a burden to the United States Government. Unfortunately, our relatives were not in a position financially, with anything close to that figure and therefore could do nothing to obtain the necessary affidavits for us to come to America. My father replied that, if the money were the only problem, it was easily solved. My father would willingly transfer $35,000 of his own money to America to satisfy the requirements of the U. S. Immigration authorities. Our relatives responded that, if we had this kind of money, we were better off remaining in Poland. The United States was just beginning to recover from the Depression, and our relatives were having a difficult time getting back on their feet. They had arrived in America at the beginning of the Depression, and soon after one of my uncles, who had managed to establish himself financially, was killed in an automobile accident. The misfortune they faced in America convinced my relatives that we should stay in Europe.

1927: LUBCZANSKI (LUBOW) family picture taken in Nowogrodek Poland.
Children from Right to left: Paul, George, Gitel, and Celia.
Front row from right to left: Father Beines, Grandfather Zvi-Hirsh Grandmother Lea,
Uncle Yankiel.Second row: Mother Beilke, Uncle Shaye, Aunt Goldie and Aunt Hanna.

During 1937 and 1938, the political events in Germany, with the "Anschluss" (*March 14, 1938 Austria is incorporated into Germany*), followed by the "Sudetenland" affair *(September 1938)* the dismembering of Czechoslovakia, brought fear to the Jews in Poland. In 1938, Poland's fear of war materialized when part of the military reserve was mobilized to put pressure on Lithuania to establish normal relations with Poland and resolve the dispute over border line adjustment, claims festering since the end of World War One. After the reserve was mobilized, the towns and villages in Poland experienced the first instance of food hoarding.

During the First World War, the front lines between Germany and Russia were only ten kilometers from Nowogrodek. The farmers were unable to bring their crops to the cities; many a city dweller experienced the taste of hunger. This time they wanted to ensure that they had sufficient food and supplies. Fear of war consumed the general population of Poland as 1939 approached. When Germany started to make demands on Poland regarding the corridor *(a slice of Polish land that separated Prussia from Germany)*, a wave of panic again gripped Poland. Since the Munich affair, *(four Powers England, France, Italy & Germany signed an accord allowing Germany to take Sudetenland*—hoping to avert war in Europe) England and France had promised to come to the aid of Poland.

Russia after the Stalin-Hitler pact *(August 23, 1939 Ribbentrop and Molotov in Moscow sign a non-aggression treaty)* was treacherously sitting on the fence. War between Poland and Germany was now probable.

Fear of war and fear of Germany were gripping the Jewish population of Poland. We had first-hand reports of the mistreatment of Jews from those Jews fleeing to Poland after being expelled from Germany. Since Nowogrodek was only 75 kilometers from the Russian border, my father, my two brothers and I were preparing to flee to Russia. We had a seamstress in our house for days sewing backpacks, clothing and anything else needed for our flight to Russia.

The local farmers predicted that war would not start at least until September. They anticipated the Germans would give them time to harvest their grain and clear the fields so that their armies could move across them freely. The farmer's predictions came true. As September approached, the noises from across the German border became louder and more threatening. Germany demanded that Poland give up the Corridor so that Germany could be united with Prussia. Poland resisted their demands and, with the support of England and France, hoped to make a stand against Germany. On September 1, 1939, in the early morning hours, and without any declaration of war, Germany attacked Poland. The war raged on in the west. The Polish Army resisted, but could not stop the advance of the German troops. They retreated toward Warsaw, the capital of Poland. About two weeks later, the German troops surrounded the capital.

Hearing the bad news from the front lines, the time came for us to leave the safety of our homes and to cross the border into Russia. Our women were to be left behind in the hope that the Germans would not mistreat them. However, on September 17, we heard rumors that the Russian Army was coming to help Poland. The rumors were followed by the announcement that the Soviet Government had decided that the Polish Government no longer existed and that the Russian Army intended to advance and occupy eastern Poland. We were relieved. Instead of our running to the Russian border, the Russians were now coming to help us. It would no longer be necessary to leave our homes and families.

Being so close to the Russian border, Nowogrodek was one of many border cities to hear the rumbling of the approaching Russian Army. The Polish authorities disbanded and left town, and so did the police. To avoid a complete collapse of order in town, the local population formed their own voluntary civil police, called "Militz". As we watched the remnants of the Polish Army leave town, we did not have to wait long for the arrival of the first group of Russian soldiers. What followed was a surprise to the elderly who remembered the ineffectual Red Army of 1921. We were amazed at the might of the new Red Army. For weeks the town of Nowogrodek was the crossroad for the advancing Red Army with thousands of men, cars, artillery, and most impressive, the tanks, which tore up the streets at every turn and knocked over telephone poles like match sticks. For weeks, the trucks left their black tread marks on the cobblestones of our streets. It seemed to us that the Red Army was invincible.

After a few weeks, life returned to normal. The Russian Government sent in their Communist organizers. Over loudspeakers it was announced that everyone was to resume his or her daily occupation. All shops were ordered to remain open and to accept the Russian ruble and the Polish zloty on an equal basis. Our schools reopened with the same teachers but with communist principals to supervise our education. The Communist Party took over the control of the city government and slowly began to reorganize the system from a private economy to a state-run economy.

Initially, the private sector operated as before with little government interference. Soon, however, they began to feel the pinch of the new system. After the first few months of Russian rule, the local businesses received tax bills with astronomical figures. When the business people complained to the Finance Department they were told that, since the prices were rising daily, and the businesses were benefiting from high profits and inflation, the government wanted its share. My father deliberated but finally decided that it was still worthwhile to be in business, even with the high tax load.

My father owned a fruit store with a combination of a candy shop and other delicacies. He was selling off some old candy, which for years had accumulated in the back room. At first my father could not understand why the Russians were so loose with their rubles. They bought everything in sight without questioning the price. Many soldiers didn't even wait for their change. This indicated to my father that things in Russia were not as good as the propaganda was claiming. Too many rubles were chasing too few items, and therefore the prices were going up. After a few more months, another tax bill arrived with even higher figures than the last one.

My father, having just paid his taxes, again went to the Finance Department to find out if there was a mistake, since the tax was out of his reach. No, this was no mistake, and he was warned that payment was mandatory. He tried to reason with them but finally understood that it was not the tax they wanted. They wanted him and other citizens out of private business. In fact, the Russians guaranteed that, if he would liquidate his shop by a certain date, they would lower the tax bite. My father quickly got the message and so did all the other business people in town. The Communists wanted an end to the private sector and sought to change the economy to their own state-run-centralized system. The heavy tax on all the private shops was intended to drive them out of business.

My father was offered a job in a state-run distribution center. He closed his business and went to work for the new system.

1935: Photo of students in Hanukkah plays Nowogrodek Poland. In the back row The fifth boy from the right is George.

Along with the economy, the school system also faced a change. The Communists considered the school their primary resource for Communist indoctrination. All former Polish schools were now being changed to Russian-speaking schools. All Jewish religious and day schools were ordered closed. I was placed in the Eighth Grade of a new ten-year Russian school. In less than six months, a new system was in place, Communist in doctrine and anti-religious in nature.

Since the division of Poland between Germany and Russia, we had a huge influx of Jewish refugees from the German side of Poland, mostly male. Similar to us, they feared the Germans and hoped to find protection on the Russian side of what was formerly Poland. As time went on, these refugees became a hopeless lot. They could not return to their former homes, which were occupied by the German Army, nor were they able to get established on their own in the new environment. While they were not starving, men who just a few months before had been well to do in their own homes now had to beg for their daily existence. Witnessing the lot of the refugees later influenced our decision to stay at home and weather the oncoming storm rather than become the new refugees in the east.

While the war in Europe was turning in favor of Germany, the Russians got involved in a small war of their own with Finland. The Russian press had daily reports from the German General Headquarters on their victories in Europe and Africa, with little commentary. It was ironic that England and the allied camp were referred to as the imperialist and enemy camp.

There were no reports on the Nazi atrocities in Poland. Some news did filter through the Russian-German border. We were aware that a Ghetto was formed in Warsaw and that some Polish territories were being incorporated into the Third Reich. We heard that the Jewish population was going through hard times. Yet the Nazis made an agreement with Russia that all German nationals might return to Germany and other nationals whose families were separated by Poland's division would also be allowed to return.

Some Jewish refugees whose families were under the German occupation did register to return to their homes. The German nationals were allowed to go to the Third Reich with all of their possessions, assisted by the German Army transports. However, this was not the case for the Jews. They were rounded up by the NKVD *(Soviet Secret Police)* and exiled to Siberia. What at the moment seemed to be a tragedy in the long run was a blessing. The German attack on Russia freed them from Siberia, and the majority survived the war, while in occupied Poland, most of their families perished in the Nazi death camps.

The treatment of the Jewish refugees by the Communists was deplorable, but this was later overshadowed by the Nazi atrocities and, as such, little was ever written about it. It was this treatment of the Jewish refugees by the Communists that later influenced our decision not to seek refuge in Russia.

The war in Finland was not over as fast as the Russians had predicted. The Finnish, with their tiny population, put up a good fight and exposed to all the weakness of the Red Army, which were noted by the German generals. The Russian people were kept misinformed, but the truth could not be hidden for long when the war casualties kept filling up the hospitals, and death notices appeared in the newspapers. It was rumored that some German generals were assisting the Finnish. While the relations between Germany and Russia were still politically correct, some Communist higher-ups questioned the behavior of Germany. Unfortunately, Stalin was so afraid of the so-called imperialist camp that he overlooked clear signs of Germany preparing for war on Russia.

We heard reports via the BBC radio broadcasts that Germany was transferring the bulk of its army to the eastern frontier and that war between Germany and Russia was no longer a question of months or weeks but of days or hours. Yet the Russian radio kept repeating assurances they received from the Germans that this was all imperialist propaganda from the enemy. The German Army, they asserted, were having summer exercises. They had been moved to the eastern frontier to keep them out of the reach of the Royal Air Force. This tragic drama was being enacted for the entire world to see, while the Russian population was kept in the dark. This was the position in which we found ourselves on the eve of the German attack on Russia.

The Friday before the war started, we were returning home late from an open-air youth dance. We noticed an unusual number of trucks assembled in a convoy in the marketplace. They were border police trucks covered with standard army tarps. We went to sleep not knowing their purpose. Shortly past midnight, they made their rounds according to a prepared list, informing all the people on the list that they were being exiled to Siberia. The men of the families to be exiled were taken at once to the local prison. The women and children were given two hours to pack in preparation for being shipped out. All during the night and into the morning hours, we heard people sobbing and crying. In the morning we found out that the NKVD, with the help of the local militia, were involved in the biggest one-night roundup of people to be exiled to Siberia. The only crimes of the exiled were their former wealth, earlier ties to the former Polish government, or an assumed untrustworthiness in the eyes of the Communist Party.

Foolishly, instead of getting prepared to meet the German onslaught, the Communists expended their energy exiling people. This was another of Stalin's many blunders. Rather than fortifying the border between Russia and Germany, he was busy transporting part of the population to Siberia. The Russians failed to recognize the extreme danger lurking across the border. Up to the last minute, they trusted the Hitler-Stalin Pact and continued to ship trainloads of grain to the Germans.

2

NAZI GERMANY ATTACKS SOVIET UNION

On June 22, 1941, on a clear Sunday morning, the Germans launched their surprise attack against the Soviet Union. It was the biggest attack yet undertaken by the German Army. We first learned of the attack when the German Air Force bombed the Russian military complex near our town of Nowogrodek. There was some damage to the military barracks, but the city itself was not touched. We turned to our radios for news from Moscow, but there was nothing about the war. Stalin and Molotov were so convinced that the Germans would not attack Russia; they failed to recognize the attack when it came. The "Blitzkrieg" began and the German army and air force were very successful. The Red Army was completely demoralized.

Our city became the crossroad of the retreating Red Army. On the second day of the war, most of the city officials left town.

It was 1939 all over again. Our family had to decide whether to remain in Nowogrodek. We feared the Germans and were ready to leave. A group of our young Jewish friends stopped over at our house and urged us on to join them and flee to Russia. This time, though, our parents were not ready to leave the comforts of their home to become refugees in the hinterlands of Russia. Nearly two years of Russian rule and the behavior of the Communist Party made the prospect of seeking refuge in Russia less desirable. While our parents would not stop us from going if we wanted to, my brothers and I decided to stay with our family and weather the oncoming storm at home.

Day after day, the mighty German Air Force crossed our city in formations numbering in the hundreds. Never in our lives had we ever seen such a display of air power. As children, we were fascinated with the roar of the planes and made a game of counting the planes on their way east and again on their way back to their bases, counting their losses. The city itself was still not touched. We were assured that our town had no military installations and therefore would be spared from destruction.

On Wednesday, June 24, 1941, we were again out in the street watching the planes go by. We heard the roar of a small formation of planes and began counting them when we noticed a couple were falling out of formation to make a quick dive toward the city. By the time we had counted 25 planes, we heard the whistling of the bombs and the ground shook from explosions. We realized then that our town was being bombed and quickly ran into our bomb shelter. The shelter was an old stone and cement basement in our neighbor's home. The shelter continued to fill up with more people as the explosions were getting closer and closer. One explosion shook the house, and all the accumulated dust was coming down from the basement ceiling. We thought that the house had been hit and fell flat on the basement floor.

After a few more explosions, things quieted down. The dust settled, and we again ventured outside. While the bombing was short, the damage was extensive. What unfolded in my sight was my first exposure to the horrors of war. I tried to cross the marketplace in order to seek shelter at the nearby cemetery.

The telephone poles and the electric wires were down. All over there were the bodies of dead or badly wounded people. Some corpses were torn apart by the blast of the bombs. You could see torn limbs of people and horses all over the marketplace. There was no one to help them. Everyone who could was leaving town for a safer place. The first bombing cost the city over 100 dead and some destroyed homes, leaving big bomb craters in the street. Our family left immediately for Pereshika, which was on the outskirts of Nowogrodek.

The news from the front was confusing. We heard that the city of Wilno was in German hands and that German tanks were near Minsk, yet Nowogrodek, which is one hundred kilometers to the west of Minsk, was still under Russian control with no Germans in sight.

The rumor mills were busy. One was that once the German Army came, they would not let you return to the city. Consequently, on Friday, June the 27, we decided to return home. The city was in chaos. The Russians were still in retreat, there was no civil authority, and there was looting of government supply houses. Anti-aircraft guns had been set up in the marketplace. A Russian Army officer to stop the looting killed one person. Anti-Semitic slogans like "Kill the Jews, Save Russia." appeared on some walls. Russian soldiers abandoned their trucks because of a lack of gasoline.

Friday afternoon, another bombing raid began over the city. This time the Germans were using incendiary bombs, igniting their targets into flames. The fire brigade no longer existed, and the fires burned freely. The wooden houses were like tinderboxes, one burning after another. Smoke appeared in the rear of our house. We tried to move some trunks out to the street, but it was too late. We could see the flames coming. Instead we grabbed our bags and ran to the outskirts of the city. The bombing continued for over an hour. From far away you could see the flames moving from street to street. By Friday evening, fire lit up the sky. When people ventured out to assess the damage the next morning, the sky was still full of smoke. The report was that half of the town was gone, burned to the ground. The heat was so intense that it melted the glass of the windows. Our house with everything in it was gone, but we thanked God that we were alive.

Nearby farmers claimed that the German Army was near the city. On Sunday, we went back to Nowogrodek. Since our house was gone, we moved into our late grandfather's old house with five other families made up of our aunts, uncles and cousins. The house overflowed with people. We slept on the floor. Some of the younger children slept in the barn. We were now refugees in our own town.

The bombing and the fire made us homeless overnight. We lost everything except for the clothing on our backs and the backpacks we took along when we left the city. It was a difficult time for all of us, especially the older ones. After a life of being the lady in her own house, my mother found it difficult to adjust to the hardship and reality of war. She complained of having to sleep in a strange bed and share the kitchen with the other women in the family. The loss of our grandfather her father in the summer of 1940 affected my mother deeply. We lived now from day to day, not knowing what the future held for us. The city was still free. The Russian Army had left town but the Germans had not marched in yet.

Some of our friends who early in the week had left Nowogrodek for Eastern Russia returned with bad news. The Old Russian border was closed, and all civilian refugees were being turned back. Only the military were permitted to cross the border. There was more bad news.

Some of our friends had lost their lives in the indiscriminate bombing of the highways by the German Air Force. For the moment we were glad that we had chosen to stay home rather than run to Russia.

On July 3, the German soldiers entered the city. The street where our grandfather's house was located was a connecting road to highways leading from Baranovich and Horodishze. The German soldiers came on their three-wheel motorcycles. There was no resistance. Everything proceeded smoothly. They crossed in front of our house, entered the driveway of the brick factory, which was owned by a German national, and disembarked in the front yard. They were followed by a few more truckloads of soldiers who proceeded to the marketplace. Soon after, the military police units arrived. The city was now firmly in the hands of the Germans.

Some of the townspeople attempted to meet the invading military. Our elders stayed inside, but my brothers and cousins and I, out of curiosity, ventured out to get a glimpse of the Germans. At the beginning, they acted humane, but as soon as they found out that we were Jews, they hit us and cursed us, so we ran home and stayed out of their way. As more soldiers crossed the city on their way to the east, they came into the Jewish homes and helped themselves to whatever they liked. It was open season to rob the Jewish homes. My mother tried to reason with them and begged them not to take our possessions, but her efforts were futile. Instead, the soldiers warned us our condition would worsen as soon as the civilian Nazis took over, saying: "For Jews under the Nazis, things to come are bad". They refused to elaborate, continuing to state that things would be bad. It did not take long for us to find this out.

3

1941—GERMAN OCCUPATION

As the German army advanced to the east, the control of the city was turned over to the civilian authorities, the Nazis ordered all the Jews to wear a yellow patch on the front and back of their clothing. Anyone caught without the patch would be arrested and punished. The "bad things to come" soon became obvious. With the help of local collaborators, the Germans made a list of all former leaders in the Jewish community under the Polish and Russian governments. Included in the list were known Communists and their sympathizers. Systematically, all those on the list were arrested and taken to the local prison by the German military police. Those arrested were not formally charged with anything, nor were there any trials. They simply "disappeared". Days after their arrest, family members began inquiring about those arrested. The German said they were all in labor camps or labor brigades helping the army to repair damaged highways and airfields. This was the beginning of the big lie.

Despite all the horror stories, no one suspected that those taken from us were already dead. To confuse and pacify us, the Germans spread rumors that the arrested men had been seen working on road repair at a designated place. Some of the wives and sisters of the arrested ones walked for days in search of their loved ones, only to return disappointed.

As we were to discover years later, all of those who were arrested were executed the next morning and buried in a mass grave in the forest of Skridleve bordering the city of Nowogrodek. This massacre was the fulfillment of one of Hitler's secret orders to the Army to liquidate the leaders in the occupied territories of Soviet Russia.

The Nazis, with the help of the German Army, took control of the city administration. The Jewish community was ordered to select a "Judenrat", a

13

Jewish advisory council, which would represent the Jewish community in dealing with the Germans. From then on, individual Jews were forbidden to communicate with or question German authorities. The Nuremberg laws pertaining to the Jews *(anti Jewish laws adopted by the NSDAP congress in Nuremberg September 15, 1935)* became the law in the occupied territories. Jewish children were barred from attending public schools, or any school for that matter. All able-bodied men and women were ordered to report daily to the Judenrat for work assignments. Assembling in the front yard of the Judenrat house, we were given our day's assignment. After the work brigades were formed, we were taken under guard to our assigned places.

My first job was to clear the rubble from the damaged official buildings. The building, which at one time housed the governor of the Polish state of Nowogrodek, had taken a direct hit of a German bomb. Our job was to remove the rubble and to begin restoration of the bombed-out building. The German guards constantly hit us with rubber hoses and leather straps, cursing us and beating us to work faster. The rubble was carried on hand stretchers and loaded onto wagons to be hauled away. Our hours were long, from sunup almost to sundown. Our reward was a piece of bread at the end of the day. In the evening, we returned under guard back to the Judenrat, occasionally being beaten on the way.

One evening the Judenrat sought volunteers from the returning workers. They had received an urgent request from the SS to bring in 50 workers to help them clean the local prison. Since most were anxious to go home after a hard day's work, not many volunteered. To induce more workers to volunteer, the Judenrat promised them an extra loaf of bread for a few hours' work in the prison. The trick worked. The group of volunteers was marched over to the local prison. One of the volunteers was a close friend of my father by the name of Mishkin. After a few hours, when the workers failed to return home, there were inquiries to the Judenrat from their families. The Judenrat assured that the men would return in the morning. Next morning, when no one returned, there were more inquiries. The SS had lied to the Judenrat. None of the men were ever seen alive again. Some families persisted in further inquiries.

1921: Market place Nowogrodek Poland. Two story buildings from right to left 1.Harkavi 2.Israelite. George and Paul were born in the basement apartment of the Israelite building. -On July 26,1941 50 Jews were publicly executed by the Nazis in this market place.

The man in charge of the local prison was a former Polish policeman by the name of Genshik. Mrs. Mishkin, who before the war had been a next-door neighbor of the policeman, went to him for information. He was polite to her, expressing his sorrow that her husband was among the missing. While he did not tell her what had happened to the workers, he advised her to forget about her husband and to go on with her life. The SS were killing the workers and keeping it a secret, but not for long.

One day my brother Paul was assigned to a group of Jews to herd cattle to the city of Baranovich. The cattle were taken from the local farmers and shipped to Germany. On the way to Baranovich, he passed the village of Horodishze. Horodishze was about half way from Nowogrodek to Baranovich. In Baranovich, after delivering the cattle, they came upon thousands of Russian prisoners of war. What they saw was horrific. The men were half starved and begging for bread and water. When the local peasant women tried to hand them food or water, the German guards opened fire in both directions, killing many women and POW's.

After this shocking event, they came upon even more horror. My brother stopped in Horodishze on his way back to Nowogrodek and realized that most of the Jewish people were gone. A local farmer told him that, all the Jews had been rounded up a couple of days before, taken to a nearby ravine, and machine-gunned. They were all buried in a mass grave. The farmer told my brother that, he would take him to the place of the mass murder. Even worse, the farmer told him the ground had continued to move for days. Many of the people had been buried alive, only having been wounded during the massacre. When they returned to Nowogrodek, my brother and friends relayed the story to the local Judenrat. They were shocked and asked the group of cattle herders to keep the horrible stories to themselves to prevent panic from spreading.

Before making inquiries of the German authorities, the Judenrat first wanted to verify the story. The Judenrat engaged two reliable men and sent them to confirm my brother's story, which was almost too horrifying to believe. The two men returned, confirming everything my brother had reported. The news traveled fast. The entire Jewish community was shocked. The Judenrat turned to the German authorities for an explanation. To its hor- ror, the Germans did not deny the killings. They claimed that the Jews of Horodishze were bad Jews who had resisted the German advance on the city and, therefore, had to be killed. They assured the Judenrat, however that the Jews of Nowogrodek were good Jews and had nothing to fear and what had happened in Horodishze would not happen in Nowogrodek.

Why we believed them then I do not know. Maybe it was too early to rec- ognize that the Germans did not need any excuse for killing. The play had just begun, and the drama was slowly unfolding.

It did not take long to shatter our illusions. On Saturday, July 26, 1941, an urgent request came from the Gestapo to supply 100 workers and assemble them in the town's marketplace. As soon as those selected entered the square, they noticed that all the side streets were being heavily patrolled by German soldiers and their local helpers. When the group reported to the Commandant for their assignments, he was visibly agitated, screamed that the Jews and everyone else had better learn to obey orders from the Germans and be punc- tual in fulfilling them. The Judenrat had been ordered to report with the workers at Noon. They were now 50 minutes late, and therefore, 50 Jews would be executed as punishment. The 100 assembled workers were scared but in a state of bewilderment, hoping that the death punishment was just a threat. However, SS Commandant Reuter did not make empty threats. He selected 10 Jews randomly from the group and marched them to the center of the marketplace. More SS men moved on the market place from all sides. He then ordered 10 soldiers to line up facing the Jews. They raised their rifles and fired, killing the 10 Jews for all assembled to see. Next they proceeded with the second, third, fourth and fifth group until all 50 Jews were executed. By the time the fourth and fifth groups were led to their slaughter, some tried to escape, only to be gunned down by the soldiers.

The remaining 50 Jews were ordered to put the dead bodies on wagons and take them to the local Jewish cemetery and bury them in one mass grave. Religious ceremony was forbidden. These remaining 50 Jews were then released, my uncle Avremel among them.

The Judenrat was ordered to bring other Jews to the market place to wash away the blood from the cobblestones. Under the threat of death, each family had to supply one worker. My mother, to spare us the horror, volunteered to go. At the market place near where the Jews had been executed, an orchestra played for the enjoyment of the SS while Jewish mothers washed away the blood of their slain children. When my Uncle Avremel returned home after witnessing the executions, his face was white like snow: When he tried to tell us what had happened, his mouth moved but the words did not come out.

This was the shock treatment that the Germans were administering to Nowogrodek and to all the other Jewish settlements in what was formerly Polish and Russian territory. After this tragedy, it became clear that the Germans killed for the sake of killing and that their threats to the Jews and the rest of the local population to be taken seriously. Little did we know then that our tragedy was just beginning. This was just the first act of the Germans' deadly play. Again the Germans assured the Judenrat that the incident was just an isolated case. As long as we were punctual in reporting to our assigned work, this would not happen again.

1935: Osher, George and Paul Ostanszynski taken
in Nowogrodek Poland. Photo was sent to relatives
in new york.

Having no choice in the matter, my brothers and I continued to report for
work. However, my father went through a period of shock. For months he

stayed hidden inside a cubicle in an abandoned shop, which was shut off from the public. As my two brothers and I worked regularly, the Judenrat left us alone.

Soon, however, the SS came up with new demands. One afternoon in August they requested the Judenrat to assemble all Jewish carpenters. Again we feared the intent of the Germans, but this time about 50 carpenters were selected and transported to the city of Baranovich to work in a carpenter shop, included in this group was my uncle Moishe.

The next act the SS arranged was extortion. First they ordered all the door-knobs made of brass or copper to be turned in to help the war effort. The doorknobs and handles were delivered as ordered. They then asked for all of our silver. The Judenrat had difficulty collecting everything, because the population began to hide things. After the first delivery of silver, the SS estimated that more than half of the utensils, candlesticks, rings, and other ornaments of the Jewish households had not been turned in. With the threat of death hanging over the head of any family that refused to comply, the Judenrat came back for another collection.

The SS was satisfied, but not for long. A few weeks later, another group of SS arrived in town with orders to collect all the gold and diamonds. Again the Judenrat, with the assistance of the local military police, went from house to house to collect the gold and diamonds. The collection was repeated three times. Each time the Judenrat delivered the coins and rings and other jewelry, the Gestapo demanded more.

They instructed the Judenrat to arrest a member of any rich Jews family that failed to relinquish their gold. The threat worked and more gold was collected. Ironically, this worked to our advantage during the collections. Our house was destroyed during the German attack on our town, and we claimed poverty, since everything we had went up in flames. Unknown to the Germans, we had buried our gold and silver during the Russian occupation and, for the present time, the elders felt that it was safer if it remained undisturbed.

As soon as the cold weather set in, the SS came to collect all of our warm boots and coats. They especially wanted fur coats and gloves. It seems that the German Army had been caught unprepared for the Russian winter.

My father, after months of isolation, gave up his cubicle and went to work. He was assigned to work in a local milk farm tending the cows. The milk farm was a former government collective farm and, when the Russians abandoned it, the Germans took it under their control.

The advance of the German Army to the east left our town in the rear, far away from the front line. The news we read in the German newspapers was disheartening. The Russian front had collapsed and the German Army was in the outskirts of Moscow. The Russian government was evacuating Moscow. The German Army was advancing on all fronts. Russia was near collapse.

The local Byelorussians were jumping on the bandwagon to land on the winner's side. Volunteers were joining the local police and guard units. Some local German nationals joined the Gestapo. The Gestapo acted as both Judge and Jury. To be arrested by them meant certain death. Their victims were tortured to extract confessions for crimes they never committed.

The town elders tried to analyze our situation. The frontline was a thousand kilometers to the east. In the west, the English were across the Channel. "Whence could our help come from?" We were trapped and left to the whims of the Nazis. We had to suffer and to endure, maybe, through a miracle, things would change.

The Judenrat was being manipulated by the Nazis; more Jews were entering the slave labor force. As long as we supplied free labor to the Germans, our existence would be justified, and therefore we would survive the war. The food situation was getting worse. Harvest time came and went. Most of the crops were taken by the Germans for their army. After the Germans took their share, the local farmers were left with little to sell. The farmers, having lived under three different governments, refused to take any paper currency, accepting only silver or gold coins. We were left to comb the fields for leftover potatoes.

The Jews who did not lose their homes and possessions to the bombings traded their material goods for food. In our case, due to the fire, we lost our house and everything in it. We were homeless and worried about the coming fall and winter.

In early 1940, soon after the Russians occupied our city, my parents decided to bury their gold, silver, and dollars in the ground for safekeeping. Every family member was present at the site and helped to dig a deep hole in the ground. Some of the coins were placed in metal containers. The paper money was stuffed into glass bottles. Everything was carefully placed in the ground then covered with earth. To ensure that all would remember the spot, a big rock was put right above the treasure and again covered with earth until the spot was level with the ground. The location of the hole in the ground was about one meter to the rear of the steps, which led to the rear entrance of our house. Our parents and grandparents had lived through World War I and realized the dangers facing all of us in wartime. Each of us made a mental note of the location so that any one of us, in case of need, would be able to locate the buried money.

The Germans had begun to take apart the bombed out housing and in many instances had come upon hidden treasures. The decision was made to dig up our money. A German Gendarme *(military policeman)* by the name of Wolfe, who had been stationed in Nowogrodek during the First World War, provided some assistance to the Jews for sufficient compensation. He offered his services in protecting us during the recovery of our hidden treasure. Gendarme Wolfe took my mother, my brother Paul and me to our burned-out house, and he kept watch while we—dug out our money.

The ground was covered with the rubble of the burned building. The wooden steps were gone, but the brick walls were still standing. Digging in the general area of the hidden money, we dug down to about four feet where the rock was supposed to be. There was no rock. We widened the hole in case we had missed the exact location. Again no luck. We were almost ready to give up but decided to dig just a little deeper. We had gone down another three feet when we finally struck the rock. The earth was soft and the weight of the silver and gold plus the weight of the rock had caused the rock and the buried gold and silver to settle deeper in the ground.

Gendarme Wolfe, true to his word, took us back to the place where we lived. We thanked him and paid him for his services. The gold and silver was now divided up among each family member. Some coins were sewn into our underwear and belts. Others were put into the heels and soles of our shoes by my Uncle Yankel, who was a shoemaker. With the money, we were able to buy food to sustain ourselves.

We slept in the barn and the nights were getting colder. Our thoughts were turning to how we would survive the coming harsh winter. The SS had already collected our warm boots, fur coats and gloves. What we did not know at the time was that the Nazis had definite plans for the Jews.

4

DECEMBER 1941—FIRST MASS SLAUGHTER— FORMATION OF GHETTO

On Friday, December 5, 1941, we were returning home from work and noticed people crowding around the kiosk to read an official notice. It proclaimed that the city of Nowogrodek would be locked up for three days. The population was ordered to prepare food and water for three days and nights. The order applied to Jew and non-Jew alike. Under penalty of death, everyone was ordered to stay inside their living quarters starting Friday at sundown. Anyone who ventured outside in the street or highway would be shot. No reason was given for the notice. The news of the official notice spread quickly, and so did the rumors.

There were rumors that farmers from the nearby villages were being recruited to dig ditches in the forest of Skridleve. The city was being surrounded by a heavy detachment of the German SS and their helpers. Despite the edict, some Jews tried to leave town on Friday night. Only a few made it. Most of them were killed, with the bodies left strewn in the street. With heavy hearts, we returned to the barn to spend another night wondering what the morning would bring.

Saturday morning, all the Jewish homes had visitors. The visitors consisted of one member of the Judenrat along with two gendarmes with official orders to be read to all members of the household. All able-bodied Jewish men and women were ordered to take provisions and clothing for three days and assemble as soon as possible in the local courthouse. The old and the children were to be left at home.

There were no children in our family. Our youngest brother Osher was 14 but looked older. It was easier for us to leave home than it was for other families. Since the bombing, all we had left was what we could carry on our backs. It was more difficult for the Jews who still had their homes.

On such short notice, what do you take with you, and what do you leave behind? Our Christian neighbors had some knowledge of what was coming. Jews made deals with their Christian neighbors to keep their possessions for safekeeping. These transactions between the Jews and Christians continued with no German interference. Others tried to take along as much as they could carry and more. Some loaded up their sleighs and pulled along more personal possessions, bringing along the women and children.

We were puzzled, the Germans did not make any attempt to stop anyone who disobeyed the order by bringing family members. Others according to the instructions, left their wives and small children home. We were told that we were being taken to a work camp. Those families with grandparents left their children with them and reported as ordered to the courthouse. The scene is still vivid in my eyes as groups of Jews slowly made their way through the street, pushing and pulling any contraption that would move.

As the gathered crowd around the courthouse grew bigger and bigger, so did the noise and confusion. We wondered where we would spend the night. The three buildings comprising the courthouse complex were not large enough to hold so many people.

It was freezing, yet they kept us outside until dark. The so-called "Einsatzgruppen" *(Special SS units)* had their plan. The low visibility was better for them. Let the Jews come to them, let them assemble peacefully; let them think that they were going to a camp to work. Why create panic and resistance? Let them bring their children; let them bring their old folks. It was all a ruse. Once evening came, the game was over.

Hundreds of the SS and their helpers appeared out of nowhere, ordering everyone into the courthouse buildings. The crowd started to push into the buildings. Children were crying. Women were screaming. Shots were being fired into the air. The Germans were cursing and screaming. If you did not move fast enough you would get hit by a rifle butt or leather belt. Where would all the people fit in? The three buildings could only hold a few hundred and now thousands were being forced inside. One three-story building housed the court chambers where trials were held. The second building was an one-story structure that housed the administration. The last building was the auxiliary and guardhouse.

After being pushed and shoved, we wound up on the top floor of the main building. The room we were placed in was once the court chamber. In normal times, it could accommodate about 40-50 people. Now it was filled with more than 400 souls. We were packed in like sardines. We could find only enough floor space to stand. The noise was overpowering. Children were crying, adults were arguing. To move around, you had to step over wall-to-wall people. There were no toilet facilities. The steps between the floors became the outhouse. They soon overflowed with human excrement. All the buildings were now under heavy guard. No communication between buildings was allowed.

We did not need the wisdom of king Solomon to understand that we could not go on like this for long. Something drastic was being planned for us. The rumor mills had it that only the young and able-bodied would be taken to work. The rest would be killed. Some bearded men faced a dilemma. Many of them were young in age, but their beards made them look older. Some decided that, in a case of life and death, they would shave off their beards. Others stood by their religious convictions and kept their beards. Some compromised by tying down their beards with a white handkerchief to minimize their size. It was a tragic scene.

I was sitting on the floor fully dressed with my coat and belt, and my axe was in my belt. Why the axe? My last job was as a lumberjack, chopping wood to stoke the ovens in the offices of the Gebeitskommisar (District Commissar) Traub. I had no profession, and the axe in my belt made me look professional. My family spent the entire night on the cold floor huddled together, fearing what the morning would bring. With the first rays of light, the court chamber took on the look of an overcrowded waiting room in a wartime train station. Everyone was sitting on bundles and waiting for the whistle of the train.

Sunday, December 7, was round up day for the rest of the Jewish population left in their homes in the city. All those who chose to stay home and not join the so-called able-bodied group now crowded in the court complex. These Jews, mostly the aged, women and children, were taken from their homes and assembled in the school of the Nazarene order. What happened during their last day and night I do not personally know.

I later had a conversation with Isaac Lagatkier, whose family was originally in the Nazarene School, but survived by a twist of fate. He and his family's ordeal started the same day as ours, except his family on Friday night decided to go into hiding in a concealed basement, to wait out the next few days.

On Saturday morning they heard all the commotion going on around them. They waited until things quieted down, and that afternoon decided to return to their home. On their way, they met a German soldier who ordered them to go back to their house and wait for him to return with instructions. When they came to the front of their house, the door was already boarded up. They removed the boards and entered the house. They stayed in the house and for the last time slept in their home.

Sunday morning they were taken from their home, and together with other Jewish people, mainly the old, the women, and children, were placed in the school building of the Nazarene order. The same chaos was going on there as in the court complex. The Germans went around collecting all victims' valuables. The Jews were ordered to give up all their gold and silver jewelry, including diamond, and watches, and valuable pieces of clothing like fur coats and hats.

The Lagatkiers worked for a German family who were part of the civilian administration of the city. The German, whose family name to the best of his recollection was Laue, liked the Lagatkiers and knowing what the round up meant went looking for them. He first went to the courthouse. Unable to find them there, he went to the Nazarene order where they looked from room to room until they found the Lagatkier family. Laue took the entire Lagatkier family and brought them to the courthouse, where for the time being they were safe.

All the Jews who were assembled in the Nazarene school were taken out on Monday morning December 8th to waiting trucks. They were driven to the nearby forest of Skridlewa, lined up on an edge of a ready made ravine and executed by the soldiers of the Einsatzgruppen.

Lagatkier remembered while they were being led out from the Nazarene school, he passed a room where the murderers, were already dividing their bounty before the killings. He saw boxes full of watches, fur coats, and other jewelry. Isaac was the only one of his family to survive the war. The rest perished in the Holocaust. He escaped the Ghetto of Nowogrudek in the fall of 1942 and joined up with a partisan group. He remained with the partisans until the Red Army liberated him in July 1944.

Monday morning brought the sound of machine guns. It seemed to come from the opposite side of town. The shooting went on with little interruption. The main entrance to our room was locked and guarded by both SS and regular army troops. We heard trucks coming into the courthouse yard. We heard people screaming and occasional gunshots. We listened, frightened at the sounds around us. We heard the shouts of Germans coming closer to our floor. They screamed, "Juden raus"(Jews out). We were trying to push against the doors, but the doors were still locked. Again we heard knocking on our doors and "Juden raus". We tried to push forward, but the doors still would not open. The soldiers from the outside were trying to break down the doors. They were finally broken open, and family by family were let out.

Our family tried to keep together but, as in a raging sea of water, people in the rear trying to get out were separating us against our will. My mother told me not to worry about her and told each of us to float on our own. I finally reached the exit. A soldier was trying to keep order. As I waited my turn, I could see the red face of the SS Commandant, Reuter. Each family was stopped in front of him. His first question was, "Beruf", your occupation. One man answered "Schneidermacher", tailor. Oh yes, we need tailors. Where is your family? His wife and children stepped forward. He motioned for them to go down. Hand in hand, watching the children they go.

I was finally face to face with the SS man. He asked me my occupation. I am a lumberjack employed by the Gebietskomisar. "Family?" "No family" I answered. He points at me to move to the right. I join a group of people already standing there. I look for familiar faces. My brothers Paul and Osher are there. I see my father and mother. I am confused. What is happening to us? Why are so many professional people being told to go down to the court-yard? They are needed, and we are left behind. Why is such a small group left behind?

My cousin Daniel is also directed to our side. His father, mother, and five children are going down. Two older soldiers are guarding us. Daniel, speaking fluent German, asks the guard for permission to go down with his family. The guard points the rifle at him and pushes him back. Daniel is persistent, he keeps asking for permission to join his family. The interaction continues for a short while. On the last attempt, the guard seems to lose his patience and lets Daniel join his family. He turned to us and remarked, *"Dummer Jude er geht zu sein tot"* "Stupid Jew, he is going to his death". This was the first indication we had that our group was to be left alive and the rest killed. Is this why the machine guns had been going all morning?

Something was pulling Daniel to go down to be with his family. Did he realize the gravity of the situation? He went down to join them. In the court-yard, he came across a German officer with whom he had been in daily contact while working in the "arbeitsamt"—employment office. He pleaded for his help in saving his family. They found the family lined up to be loaded onto the truck. Daniel, with the help of the officer, was able to lead the family of eight to safety, saving them from imminent death.

After the selection, we are ordered back into the room. Again the image of a train station, but now the train has left and so have most of the passengers, except for their baggage. There are bundles all over. We hear the cry of a baby. We searched through the bundles of clothing and found the infant. But where are the parents? Did they pick up the wrong bundle, or was the baggage too much of a liability to be taken along? We are looking for a bottle for water to quiet down the infant. The water helps, the infant stopped crying. Now, is it our turn to cry?

My two Abramovitz cousins are left alone—their father, mother and sister are gone. My second cousins, Polonskis, are saved, but their father, mother and sister are gone. Few women are left. I am relieved and glad to have my mother, father and brothers. Looking around, I see we are the only family left intact. All the rest are only remnants of families.

My cousin Yehoshua wants us to lift him up on our shoulders so he can reach the high window overlooking the yard. We keep him on our shoulders and he describes what he sees. There are many trucks in the courtyard, and people are being pushed into them. Some hesitate, one man refuses to go. Oh my God, he is shot. One older man understands what is happening. He is wrapped in his prayer shawl and is reciting his last prayer. More shots are fired. We lower my cousin down.

Funny how big the room looks now, each bundle a memorial to a family. Are we the lucky ones? Or are they? Our pain is just beginning, theirs will soon be over. The reality sinks in. Now we cry. The constant sound of machine-guns, when will it stop? This is Monday, December 8, 1941—*(Dec.7, Hawaiian time)*—a day of infamy for the Jews of Nowogrodek.

This is our Pearl Harbor. A date the survivors will always remember as the first *"Aktion"* mass slaughter of Jews in Nowogrodek.

It is Monday December 8, late in the afternoon. The machine guns stopped. Now it is our turn. Again, shouts of *"Juden raus"* are heard. We are being taken down to the courtyard, under heavy guard. The Commandant of the SS Reuter tells us not to worry. We are safe. A section of the city of Nowogrodek will be fenced in to make a Ghetto. The Christian population will be moved out. They, in exchange, will receive the homes of the Jews in the city. The surviving Jews will live in the Ghetto in the suburb of Pereshike. Our job for this night is to disassemble the fence from the horse market, take it section by section on our shoulders and bring it across town to the Ghetto in Pereshike. There the fence will be reassembled to enclose the Ghetto.

It is a cold wintry night; each section of the fence is covered with frozen ice and weighs a ton. Twelve men are assigned to each section, six on each side. We lift the heavy burden and put it on our shoulders. The men on each side are not evenly matched. The taller ones bear a disproportionate share on their shoulders. One short man runs from side to side to help us. Each time he gets hit by the German SS for not putting his shoulder under the section of the fence. It is fun for the SS, but it is a tragic for the rest of us. It took us until midnight to reassemble the fence around the Ghetto.

Tuesday morning, we were marched through town under guard to the Ghetto. There were new rules and orders. No Jew may walk by himself to town. We were to be taken to work every day under guard and returned the same way in the evening. A guard station was erected at the entrance to the Ghetto, manned by the Byelorussian police.

The first night in the Ghetto, the survivors assemble in our house for an evening prayer. We were all bereaved. My mother lost her brother Yankiel with his family, and her mother Lea, my only living grandma, who had helped to raise us. The entire population was in mourning. Everyone stands up to recite the "Kaddish" prayer for the dead. The final count of the massacre revealed that from over 6000 Jews, only about a 1000 have survived. The selection was erratic. One building was passed up for selection. Rumor had it that the Judenrat whose families were housed there bribed the SS. In our building, about ten percent survived after the selection. From the third building, there were no survivor's—all were taken to the trucks, transported to the forest and killed. No one returned from the forest. All were killed and buried in a mass grave.

There was no longer any denial that the Germans intended to exterminate us all. This time we were lucky and had survived, but for how long?

The question being asked in modern days is, why was there no resistance? First of all, the Jews had no standing army to defend us. Even Poland, France, and all the other European countries with their artillery and Air Force did not last but a few weeks against the might of the German army. Plus the local population refused to help us and in many instances participated in the crimes. At the very least, they robbed us. At the most, they were willing aides in our murders.

For centuries, the Jews had survived in the pale of Russia, not by force but by turning the other cheek. Any time the younger ghetto survivors brought up the question of resistance, our elders warned that resistance would hasten our destruction. In hindsight we could have killed more Germans and maybe saved a few lives. At first no one believed that the Germans would kill for the sake of killing.

Family ties kept many of us from running away. To abandon your mother and father and family and save yourself was not the Jewish way of thinking. Later on, when the families were already broken up, people were more inclined to escape and try to save themselves.

What was our state of mind after the first mass killing when we knew that the same thing could happen to us? In order to maintain your sanity, you imagined, yes, there would be a killing, but someone else will be killed. I will survive. You may call it self-denial, but this is how the human mind works.

When we finally realized that everyone would be killed, our way of thinking changed. We looked for any way to escape and save ourselves. Our first organized effort to join the underground was made right after the first mass killing. The only active partisan group at that time was the Polish AK *(Armja Krajowa)* home army. A group of young men from our Ghetto of Nowogrodek went to the Naliboker Forest. They had arms and wanted to join the Polish underground. They were disarmed and sent back to the Ghetto with instructions Jews were not welcome. Later on, when the Russian Partisans were organized, individual Jews were accepted in their unit. Women and children were kept out. Finally, when the Bielski Brothers, a local Jewish family, formed a Jewish Partisan unit they accepted women and children. Thanks to their efforts, more than a 1000 Jews were saved from Hitler's final solution.

After the Ghetto was formed, my brother Paul was assigned to work in the nearby military complex. His job was to sort the abandoned Russian ammunition. In the process he took apart a Russian gun and piece-by-piece smuggled it into the Ghetto. The Judenrat got wind of it. The Jewish Ghetto Police arrested Paul. My mother was upset and went to the Judenrat to demand his release. She created a scene. To pacify her they released my brother, but confiscated his gun. Paul had to promise that he would stop smuggling guns.

The argument of the Judenrat was that my brother's activities, if discovered by the German authorities, would endanger the existence of the Ghetto. The SS dealt harshly against any sign of resistance.

The punishment of smuggling soon came to fruition. A local farmer in contact with a Jewish butcher was smuggling meat into the Ghetto. The farmer would throw a shoulder of beef over the fence. The Jewish butcher would retrieve the meat and sell it to the Ghetto residents. One day the Byelorussian guard noticed what was happening. The farmer dropped the meat and run. Inside the Ghetto no one dared to pick it up. This incident was reported to the District Commissar Traub. Next morning all the members of the Judenrat were invited to his office. He read to them his proclamation. Because they disobeyed a German order by allowing meat to be smuggled into the Ghetto, all of them would die. The condemned members of the Judenrat were taken to the local prison and executed.

Orders were given to the Jews in the Ghetto to elect a new Judenrat. No one was willing to serve on the council. Under the threat of more executions, a new list was presented, among them the son of the Lubczer Rabbi.

I was assigned to a brigade of Jewish workers who were taken under guard to the city to collect all the furniture from the former Jewish homes. The better furniture was cataloged and later shipped to Germany. The winter cold made our work even harder. I remember wrapping my shoes with newspaper and towels to keep out the cold.

The German officials were housed in the residences of the former Polish governor of the state of Nowogrodek. The buildings of the former Polish colony had running water but the pipes were frozen due to the severe cold weather. The Judenrat was ordered to provide laborers to work around the clock to find and defrost the frozen sections of pipe. The ground was frozen solid and in order to find the pipes we had to dig through the ice. We had to maintain a 24-hour fire to thaw the ground to reach the pipes.

While the German Army had scored a big victory in the summer, with the coming winter and intense frost, they suffered their first defeat near Moscow. General Staff Hase came to Nowogrodek to rest and regroup. On Christmas Eve 1941, the District Commissar Von Traub, General Hase, and a few others of their fellow officers were celebrating the holiday. They had some drinks and came outside for fresh air. They came upon the working Jews tending to fires and asked them if they were coming back tomorrow to work. They answered yes.

The Germans were having fun as the three young Jews continued their work. For no apparent reason, and without warning, the German officers drew their guns and shot the three Jews. Their bodies were dragged over to the burning fire and left there to be consumed by the flames. The Germans watched the fire for a while until they grew bored and returned to their quarters.

Two of the Jews were killed instantly, but Kushner, the third one, was only wounded. He had passed out from the initial shock of the bullet, but the heat of the fire revived him. He played dead until the Germans returned to their quarters, then slowly crawled away to find the group of Jews working a couple of blocks away. He told them what had happened. They tended to his wound, covered him with a warm coat, and hid him until morning.

The Judenrat in the Ghetto was notified of the incident. They arranged for a horse and sleigh and transported Kushner back to the Ghetto. Surprisingly, the Germans took an interest in his recovery. He was allowed to visit the local clinic run by Jewish doctors for the benefit of the general population. In time Kushner recovered from his wounds, only to be killed later, during the mass escape from the camp.

This shooting of the three Jewish men may seem insignificant in comparison to the mass murder we had witnessed just a short while before. But unlike the other killings, this was not part of a systemized plan. Someone in the higher echelons of command did not order this killing. This killing was simple murder by three Nazis who killed for their own excitement. Those same people later claimed that all they did was follow orders from higher-ups.

The German authorities were now in full control of our lives in the Ghetto. Following their orders, the Judenrat had set up a Jewish Police Force whose primary objective was to keep order inside the Ghetto. On the outside, the German SS guarded the Ghetto with their Byelorussian helpers. The main gate of the Ghetto had a permanent guardhouse staffed by the same SS people. Daily we were marched from the Ghetto to the city under guard to our assigned work places.

In the spring of 1942, I was reassigned to work in a local tannery. It employed the former Jewish owner supervised by an Aryan assigned by the German authorities. The production methods were primitive the work was hard. The smell of skins and chemicals was overpowering. Still I was glad I had the job, believing that my life would be spared if I were needed as slave labor.

One day a detachment of police with the Commandant Reuter came to the factory. We were all ordered outside. Upon leaving the factory, each of us was hit in the back of the neck by an SS man who was hidden behind the door. I fell to the ground like a stunned animal. After the initial shock, we were ordered to line up in the street in front of the factory.

The Commandant read a complaint accusing the Jewish factory employees of secretly engaging in the production and sale of leather skins to the local farmers. The SS produced a man who testified that the former owner had made the deal with him. In truth, the Aryan supervisor was the one who was making shady deals, but who better to blame than the Jewish workers? We were allowed to go home to the Ghetto and ordered to report back in the morning to hear our punishment. The Judenrat was instructed to make sure all of us returned to work the next day as ordered. Our lives were in jeopardy.

No other worker would take our place, and the Judenrat insisted that all of us return to face the punishment. It was a long night for me. In the morning, I said my goodbyes to my crying family. Under guard, the group of workers was escorted back to the factory.

In the street in front of the factory, two rows of about ten SS men were lined up. The few women among us were let into the factory. The men were lined up facing the SS soldiers. The Commandant stepped forward and read us the verdict. For violating the law and selling leather illegally to the farmer, all of us would be punished with 25 lashes. Faced with the threat of death, 25 lashes were a relief. The Commandant asked for volunteers to be the first to get their punishment. No one moved. I stepped forward to get it over with. He looked at me and temporarily set me aside and then went to the column and made his own selection.

I remember the first man, Jaffe, he was ordered to walk through the lineup of the SS men who mercilessly hit him with their leather straps until he bled. Watching the punishment meted out, I realized that the faster you moved, the less you got hit. When my turn came, I ran fast with my head down. I got hit mostly on my back. The women in the factory, to add insult to injury, were hit on the behind. The pain and the marks on my back were visible for weeks. Before we were returned to the Ghetto, a rumor had been spread that we had been killed. The emotional strain on our families was greater than our physical punishment. The scars on my back eventually healed, but the emotional trauma lingered on.

5

ROUNDUP OF JEWS FROM THE DISTRICT OF NOWOGRODEK INTO THE GHETTO

SECOND MASS SLAUGHTER AUGUST 7, 1942

The Germans, in order to pacify the survivors and create a false sense of security, spread rumors that we will be spared if we work as slave laborers. We are afraid to answer the question deep down in each person's heart. If our work was so important to the German war effort, why had they previously killed so many able-bodied and highly skilled men?

The four men in our family were taken daily to their work place in the city. My brothers Paul and Osher were working at the military barracks in the nearby village of Skridleve. My father was employed on the city milk farm, and I continued with my work at the tannery. My mother was allowed to stay in the Ghetto and tend the house for our orphaned cousins and us.

The news from the big cities of Wilno, Lida, and Baranovich was bad. The same mass killing perpetrated in our town was being carried out on even a larger scale in the big cities.

Surprisingly, the Jews in some of the small towns near Nowogrodek were temporarily left alone, but not for long. In the spring of 1942, the SS organized a mass roundup of the Jews in the small towns and villages near Nowogrodek. I was home in the Ghetto. I had walked out in front of the house to get some fresh spring air when I overheard distant noises, the banging of pots and pans, the sound of people and horses. At first it sounded like a marching army, but the clearer the noise became, the less orderly it sounded. I walked toward a small hill in front of the house, climbed to the top, and turned my head to the direction of the clamor. What I saw was a sweeping panorama of people coming toward the Ghetto.

The picture reminded me of the description of the Jews being exiled to Babylon. Men and women, young and old, loaded up with bundles of clothing, pots and pans hanging from their belts.

The SS and their local helpers, surrounded all, guns pointed toward the crowd slowly being driven into the Ghetto of Nowogrodek. Suddenly, from the crowd, I heard the voice of a young girl calling my name. I looked for a familiar face but could not find one. I later learned that it was my very first girl friend that I had not seen for more than a year. She recognized me while I was standing on top of the hill looking out toward the mass of people and she called my name.

Most of the Jews were from the small towns of Lubcz, Karelitz, and Vsielub. On two hours' notice, they were told to pack up, taking only what they could carry, leave their homes, and walk to the Ghetto of Nowogrodek, a distance close to 20 km. For two days they were driven on foot toward our Ghetto, stopping from time to time for a rest. Overnight they slept in the open fields, surrounded by the SS and the local police. On their way they were joined by more Jews from the smaller villages throughout the region of Nowogrodek.

In one day the Ghetto more than doubled in population. Each household, already crowded, had to accommodate the newcomers. Again we were puzzled. Not long ago, our city had experienced the mass slaughter of Jews and the murder of many able-bodied men and women. Now the Ghetto was being filled up with old men and children. We sensed another killing in the offing. We reasoned the Nazis calculated that it was safer to bring all the Jews to the Ghetto, where they could be subordinated, than to kill them in the small towns so close to the forest where some might escape and hide. The Germans began issuing work I.D. cards to those who worked on jobs. We all received our work I.D. cards, sometimes referred as "Lebensschein" (certificate for Life), except for my mother who had no job and stayed all the time in the Ghetto.

Many times during the summer, when I came back from work to the Ghetto, I found my mother sitting on a broken-down wooden chair and crying. She carried on a conversation with God. "God", she prayed, I know the danger facing us, but please, dear God, take me and spare my children. You took my brother, his wife, and two daughters. You took my mother. Take me, but save my children. It sounded to me as if she was making a bargain with

God. I tried to break her trance and soothe her by pointing out that she still had us, but her reply was, how could she live when her mother, brother, and his family were all dead? Realizing my mother was at risk, because she wasn't working, and had no I.D. card, my father arranged with a friendly Christian to hide her in the event there was another selection and mass murder. We did not have to wait long.

On August 6, 1942, while I was at work at the tannery, we received word that the Ghetto was being surrounded by a heavy detachment of SS and their Estonian and Lithuanian helpers. In accordance with the prearranged plan, my mother left the Ghetto and headed toward her hiding place. On the way she stopped at the factory to see me. She handed me one of my grandmother's shoes, which had gold coins hidden in the soles. She hugged me and kissed me as if she knew that it was for the last time.

Although her own life was in more peril than mine, she disregarded her own safety to ensure my survival.

After she left, I broke down and cried like never before. A sea of tears was running down my face for almost an hour. The atmosphere in the factory was gloomy. My co-worker, Shelubski, approached me with the idea of escaping, to run to the nearest forest and save ourselves. My emotions were still unraveled. I could not decide on a moment's notice. Shelubski jumped out through the rear window of the factory and left. I stayed behind with the rest of the workers, awaiting our uncertain future. In my mind I began to plan for many eventualities. Should the German guard take us in the direction of the prison, I would make a run for it and try to escape, even if it meant certain death. Fortunately, when we were led out from the factory we were taken to the courthouse building, the same building where I had survived the first selection. Once in the building, we were told that this would be converted into an *"Arbeitslager"*, a forced labor camp. The court complex was fenced in with barbed wire. The main building was transformed into workshops and the auxiliary building became our barracks. As the court complex was being converted into a forced labor camp, the Ghetto was being liquidated. I was the only one of my family in the *"Arbeitslager"*, unaware of what was happening to the rest of them.

All those with work identification cards were assembled in the labor camp. All other workers were taken back into the Ghetto, which was now heavily guarded. The Jews inside realized what was coming. Many had prepared underground bunkers to hide themselves. However, the capacity of the bunkers was limited, and a drama of who should go in and who should be left out was repeated at each of them. The summer night was short. In the morning, all the Jews in the Ghetto were ordered out of their homes and required to assemble in the yard in front of the gate. As soon as they were assembled, they were ordered to lie face down on the ground. Once on the ground, they were told not to raise their heads or they would be shot. Trucks were waiting in front of the Ghetto gate. One by one, the Jews were loaded onto trucks and taken to a nearby ravine in the village of Litovke. Once they got off the trucks, they were ordered to walk in a single file to the edge of a ravine, where they were machine-gunned by the SS and fell row upon row into the ravine. The shooting went on for an entire day. Again, thousands of Jews from the Ghetto were killed. August 7, 1942 will be remembered by the survivors as the second mass killing of Jews in Nowogrodek.

The head of the Judenrat, Izikowitz, and his interpreter, Burstein, who witnessed the roundup, survived and were brought to our labor camp. Burstein was once my tutor and knew my family. I asked him if any of my family were in the Ghetto. He thought for a while then answered that none of my family was there, but almost instantly he corrected himself and said that my mother, with a small child, was delivered by a policeman near the end of the day and was taken on the last truck to be killed. I was devastated by the news. I still did not know the fate of my father and brothers, since they were being held at the military barracks in Skridleve. How my mother was discovered in her hiding place, I don't know. The man who had hidden them later told us that the German police discovered their hiding place because of the small child's crying. Others claimed that a neighbor led the police to their hiding place. The true story went with my mother to her grave. For three days, I bore the burden of our tragedy by myself.

After three days, the workers from the military complex were divided into two groups. One group formed a construction labor camp in an area of the former Ghetto. The second group including my father and my two brothers were brought into the labor camp. We were relieved and glad to see each other. For three days, they had been kept in a horse stable at the military complex in Skridleve. They experienced another selection where family members were torn apart. My brother Osher and my cousin Isaac were taken out with the group to be killed. They were both young and innocent. My cousin Paula realized they were being led to their deaths and searched desperately for a way to save them. From a distance she recognized one of the Germans who was guarding the doomed group, whom she earlier had befriended. She ran over to the German guard and begged him to release her brother and her cousin

Osher. The German guard let Osher and Isaac cross over to the group destined to be kept alive. When the group to be killed was driven out from the military complex, a few of the Jews attacked the guards and attempted to escape. They managed to wound one of the guards but, not having any weapons, they soon were overpowered and killed instantly. This drama was played out in full view of the surviving Jews.

The surviving group of Jews, including my father, brothers, and cousins, were driven into a horse stable in the military base where they were kept for three days and nights without a proper supply of food and water. This was August 1942, the warmest month of the year. While the lack of food was bearable, the people were soon dehydrated from the lack of water. They begged the guards to give them water. The guards were willing to oblige, at a price. They traded water for gold and diamonds. A cup of water was given to the group. The question arose how to divide a cup of water among hundreds of thirsty people. A committee was formed and the weakest in the group were allowed to put a finger in the cup of water and lick it off.

On the third day of their captivity, the German guards opened a small window and threw in a loaf of bread. The hungry throng of people threw themselves on the bread, to the delight and cruelty of the Nazis. The bread was torn to crumbs and trampled under their feet. The constant degradation had resulted in civilized people taking on the characteristics of animals. This led the elders of the group to impose a strong rule—not to give in to temptation but allow a few selected people to handle the distribution of the bread. When more food and water were given to the inmates, regardless of their hunger and thirst, the elected leaders in an orderly fashion handled the distribution.

While this group of Jews, which included my father and brothers, was kept in the military horse stable, the others and I were assembled at the courthouse complex. I could not bring myself to tell my father about my mother's death. Two days later, my father received the tragic news from the man who had hidden her. Now we all cried together. My father took her death very hard, carrying on and crying all day. My mother's caring and friendship was the glue that had held the family together. Now the family was broken and our lives saddened. The labor camp did not allow us the privilege of observing the traditional days of mourning, nor were we the only ones to suffer such a great loss. But life must go on.

My father did not want us to worry about him any more, since he had lived half of his life. He wanted my brothers and I to concentrate on saving ourselves. All our efforts were now directed at finding a way to escape. We all knew staying in the labor camp meant we would be killed sooner or later. Escape was our only hope of survival.

Miraculously, a small group of young children survived the latest slaughter and were smuggled illegally into the forced labor camp. The children were placed in an old abandoned basement with a couple of grandmothers to take care of them. The entrance was locked with an old rusted chain. The Germans must have known about the children, but for a while looked the other way.

One morning about four weeks later, all the camp inmates were ordered to assemble in the courtyard. The Commandant arrived with a group of SS men and went to the abandoned cellar and cut the chain. They opened the door and ordered all the children and grandmothers into a waiting truck outside the courthouse. The children cried, asking for their mothers. In the back of the first row where others and myself were lined up, stood a couple whose 3-year old was among those taken to the truck. When the child cried,"Mamma, Mamma", the mother could not restrain herself and stepped forward to run to her child. I lived through "hell and back," but this was the most painful scene to witness. We grabbed the mother and held her back while her child was taken away. Our thinking was why give the Nazis another victim? But to this day I question whether we deprived the child the comfort of her mother on her last journey of life.

In another row, an inmate who was by profession an electrician watched his two small children led away with their grandmother (his mother). He personally knew the commandant, for whom he did occasional work. He stepped out of line and ran up to Reuter and begged him to spare his mother and his children. Reuter was willing to let his mother off the truck, but refused to release the children. The son asked his mother to come off the truck, but she refused saying where the children go, she would go. That same day all of them, the children and grandmothers, were killed. To this day I battle with the moral question who was right or who was wrong? Us? The mothers? Or grandmothers.

6

PAUL'S FAILED ESCAPE FROM THE LABOR CAMP

Early in our captivity, prior to the time triple bunks were constructed in the forced labor camp barracks, many of us slept on the ground in the open air of the courtyard. I lay gazing at the stars, using a stone as a pillow, looking for a staircase to heaven to stop the moon and prolong the night. The night was a temporary refuge from the realities of the coming days, since most of the killing was carried out during daylight hours. Where are the miracles of the past, we asked ourselves? Is God aware of what is happening to us? We soon realized that in order to save ourselves we would have to initiate the action. Only then could we expect God to help us. We could not sit and wait for God to do all the work.

Until now, many of us had stayed in the Ghetto or the camp because of family ties. After the last mass murder, almost all the families had been broken up. My cousins, the Polonskis, after losing their parents, were the first to leave the camp and join the underground. Their father had been a horse trader before the war, and the boys used to accompany him on trips in the surrounding villages. They were good horsemen and their knowledge of the general area around the villages came in handy when they joined the Bielski Partisan group. They were good fighters and did not miss a chance to fight the Nazis to avenge the death of their parents. They urged my brothers and me to join them. My cousin Yehoshua took their advice, left the camp, and joined the underground.

In the early days when the camp was formed, escape was easier. Every morning a group of inmates was led to a well outside the camp to bring in drinking water. It was our only remaining contact with the outside. The guards looked the other way while the Christian population traded food for the Jewish gold and diamonds. At the same time, the Partisans were able to smuggle themselves into the camp to organize escape parties.

While the example of our cousins and their friends encouraged many to leave the camp and join the underground, many of our elders still feared leaving the so-called "security" of the camp for life in the forest. It was all right, they argued, in the summer, but what would happen when winter came? How would they survive in the open in temperatures well below zero? The winters in our part of the country were extremely cold. What we did not know then but learned later is that you can survive in the open if you know how to adapt yourself to the elements. Just like the Eskimos in the north, if you dig an underground bunker and cover it with twigs and earth and snow, the temperature in the bunker is constant and bearable. In the end, none of the Partisans died from the elements. The only casualties they sustained were in fighting the Nazis.

Small escape parties were organized daily. The escape route was directed toward the outhouse, where the coming and going of people would not arouse the suspicion of the camp patrol guards. Most escapes were carried out toward evening. The young women in our camp would flirt with the guards at the gate to keep them occupied and away from the rear of the camp. Initially, the campgrounds were surrounded with a barbed wire fence. It was easy to see the position of the guards and avoid them. We lifted the bottom wires off the ground and, one by one, the escape parties left. For a time, the escape efforts proceeded smoothly, until one evening when an escape was discovered and the guards opened fire on the fleeing inmates. Those already on the outside managed to get away, but a few were wounded and caught in the barbed wire. The SS was alerted and they came into the camp. The surviving men who had tried to escape were tortured. First they were ordered to dig their own graves, and then they were mercilessly beaten. Their legs were broken; they were thrown into the graves, and buried while still alive. This bestiality was a warning by the SS to deter any future attempts at escape.

As the weeks went by, the SS decided to put a wooden fence in back of the barbed wire to block the camp view to the outside. This made it more difficult to observe the position of the guards. It also made it difficult for the guards to see us. Finally the SS made window-size openings in the fence so the guards could look into the camp. Escape became more difficult, yet we did not give up the idea of freedom. Only the method changed.

We had a secret radio receiver in camp, and the news was encouraging. The Germans were losing on all fronts, but one thing was clear to us, even in defeat the Germans would kill us. To survive we must escape from the camp.

The first plan discussed was to organize an attack on the guardhouse, break open the gate and let as many as possible escape. Although we had smuggled guns and grenades into camp, our ammunition was limited. However, we hoped that the element of surprise would enable many to escape. We understood there would be casualties, but the fighting group was ready to sacrifice to save some of us. All proceeded according to plan, and a date and time were selected for the attack.

The majority of the camp supported the plan, but a group of about 50 women opposed it. They contended the men with guns would succeed in escaping, but they and other unarmed inmates would perish at the gate. The plan of open rebellion was put on hold.

One escape route remained available—to separate yourself from the inmates while being let out each morning to go to the well for water. There were four men in our family. My father, my brother, Osher, who was 15, myself, just past my 17th birthday, and Paul, who was 18. It was time for us to make a move.

Paul was the first to leave camp, together with my cousin Pejsach, whose brother Yehoshua was already in the underground with a Partisan group. On a prearranged day in December 1942, they left with a group of other young people from our camp. They had planned to proceed to a safe house on the outskirts of the city. There they would wait until night, when the partisans would pick them up and take them to the forest.

After leaving the camp, they proceeded in the direction of the safe house in Brichinke. The local dogcatcher owned the house. In December, the area is almost entirely covered with snow. To avoid detection, the group decided not to use the roads but to walk across the open fields. In one field, unknown to them and completely covered with snow was a narrow stream. They all stepped into the stream and their shoes and socks were soaked. Their feet were wet and cold, and it was difficult to maintain circulation, but as long as they continued to walk, the conditions were bearable.

Finally, upon arriving at the safe house, they learned of another calamity. The partisans were not coming as prearranged because a German army roadblock was set up, not far from the safe house. For this reason, the farmer refused to let them into his house but offered them the barn.

My brother soon realized that, with their wet feet and the cold weather, they were in trouble. He went back to the farmer's house and asked permission to stay inside. The farmer refused to let him in, but my brother persisted and kept knocking on the door. The farmer, unable to sleep, finally tired of my brother's knocking and let him into the house. Without a hideout, in the morning, the group of the young Jews, including my brother and cousin, returned to the forced labor camp. They waited by the well and joined the inmates on their return to the camp. We were disappointed to see them back. They were our hope in pioneering our own escape.

Unfortunately, the cold weather had taken its toll. When we tried to remove my cousin Pejsach's shoes, we found they were frozen solid to his feet. We used a knife to cut the shoes away and placed his feet in water to thaw the ice. His feet soon swelled to double their normal size. We realized then that we were dealing with severe frostbite. Luckily for my brother, because of his insistence on staying in the farmhouse, he only had frostbite on his big toe. My cousin Pejsach was in terrible pain. As the days and weeks dragged on, we had to amputate his toes in order to save his life. He was kept hidden from the German guards. He was left lying in a bunk covered with bedding. Secretly we received an ointment developed by the Germans to treat their soldiers for frostbite. It helped the healing but it was slow and painful. After liberation, my cousin had to undergo a series of operations to clear up his infected feet.

When they were unable to locate the escapees, my cousin Yehoshua and his Partisan friends were disappointed. They were also furious that my brother and cousin had not waited for another day for them. After learning of their condition, though, they understood. This early mishap, however, did not change our plans to try again.

While we in the family were planning the escape, the Germans had their own plan. We woke up in the morning of February 4, 1943 to find the entire camp surrounded with a heavy detachment of SS and their helpers. We were sure our end was near. The atmosphere of the camp was tense. We tried to revive our plan of attack, even though the odds appeared to be less favorable than before. The plan was set in motion. At the first sign of liquidation, we would attack. Early in the morning, the Commandant appeared and spoke to the leaders of our camp, assuring them that we had nothing to fear. The other camp in the former Ghetto was being liquidated because it had been discovered that the Jews were digging a tunnel to escape to the underground. While the news placated us temporarily, it brought additional sorrow. Most of us had family members in the other camp. We also knew we would be the next ones killed. The need to escape the camp became desperate.

The morning after the camp in the Ghetto was liquidated, one survivor showed up in our camp. He told us the tragic story. He claimed that he had run away while they were being led to their death. He had hidden in the forest and in the morning came through the wire fence into our camp. We asked him to show us the spot in the fence where he entered the camp so we could go and cover his footsteps in the snow.

Surprisingly, we could not find any sign of footsteps. His explanation was the wind might have blown snow over his footsteps. His story was suspicious, but since we were not able to investigate thoroughly at the time, we let him remain. Each time the inmates were called out on *"appel"*(roll call) in the courtyard, the surviving Jew from the other camp hid himself in the barracks, since his presence in the camp was illegal. While we were out on *"appel"*, the Gestapo used to search the barracks. We feared he would be discovered, but they always came out without him. Something strange was going on. The survivor's story just did not ring true, and we had many unanswered questions about his sudden appearance. How did the Germans find out about the tunnel in the Ghetto? And who told them about it? It was time to find out the truth.

A committee of three was appointed to interrogate the man. They took him down into the basement of one of the buildings and questioned him. They told him he was under suspicion and that he had better confess, or they would turn him over to the Germans. He broke down and told them the truth. He had come from a small village near Nowogrodek. When the Germans were killing all the Jews, in the village he begged them to spare him and in return he would become an informer. He was planted in the camp in the Ghetto, and it was he had who informed the Gestapo about the tunnel.

Later he was planted in our midst to inform on our plans and us. He told us that each time the inmates were called out on roll call, the Germans would question him inside the barracks about our plans in the camp.

After his confession, he was killed on the spot and buried in the basement. On the last *"appel"*, when the Germans could not find him, they asked for him. Since technically he did not exist, they soon gave up and never mentioned him again.

The return of my brother and his friends was discouraging, not only to us but also to other inmates who were planning to escape. The winter elements also had forced another person to return from the outside. Norman Shulman, who had lost his entire family in the first mass killing in Nowogrodek, had left the camp in the summer of 1942. He had known many farmers with whom he did business before the war. He had attempted to find one who would be willing to provide a hiding place for him. Most of them refused to give him shelter. They offered him food, but advised him to move on. He spent the daytime in the forest and on some nights he used to sneak into the various farmers' barns to sleep. He never spent too much time in one place for fear of being recognized and then informed on to the local authorities. With the coming of the winter, the barns did not provide enough shelter from the weather. For a few nights he slept next to the cows to keep himself warm. His condition became unbearable. With no farmer willing to take him in, he was forced to return to the camp.

This episode of Norman returning to camp after being on the outside for months, plus my brother's return, reinforced the arguments of some of the elders that we had no choice but to stay in the camp and wait for a miracle.

My father, though, was convinced that we had to actively work to survive and continued to search desperately for a place for us to hide when we made our next attempt to escape.

With the German defeat at Stalingrad, we knew that our end could come at any moment. My father looked for new ways for us to escape. He was negotiating through another Jewish family in camp, with a sympathetic farmer to provide shelter for us in the event our escape was successful.

7

ESCAPE FROM LABOR CAMP—FEB.18, 1943

By the beginning of 1943 it had become clear the Germans intended to eventually kill all the inmates in camp. Having managed to survive three mass killings, we felt our luck was running out. The only way to survive was to try to escape. We could join the underground, which was already active in our area, or find a sympathetic farmer who would shelter us until spring. By then, surely one of the Allied armies would liberate us. Chances of escaping were slim. One would have to go through or over the barbed wire, over the wooden fence and then cross a deep trench. Doing all this while remaining out of sight of the guard on the tower which overlooked the entire camp.

My father was negotiating, through another family in the camp, with a sympathetic farmer to provide shelter for us in the event our escape was successful. It was well known among the inmates that my father had gold and was willing to pay for the survival of his family. For this reason he was approached by Mrs. Dalton with a plan of escape. To assure the success of our escape, my father bribed one of the watchmen at the front gate of our camp with 50 rubles gold to let us leave.

All the arrangements were negotiated between my father and Mrs. Dalton. She was to notify us when everything was ready. In the meantime, my father was given a letter from a Jewish couple, the Bensons, who were already in hiding at the Jarmolowitz farm. They had already placed their 1-year-old daughter in a convent with the help of her sister who was married to a Christian.

Satisfied that their daughter was in safe hands, they arranged with Jarmolowitz to live on his farm. At first, the Bensons shared the house with the Jarmolowitz family, but they soon realized living in the open, even in the remote farm village of Kuscino, was not safe. Therefore, they decided to build a bunker under the barn. A personal friend of the Bensons, Joselevitz a single man, soon joined them in the bunker. To entrust our lives to Jarmolowitz was in itself a risk, since it was known he did not speak kindly of the Jews. However, our options were limited, and we agreed to the plan.

First my brother Paul and Misha, Mrs. Dalton's son, would leave camp. We would follow. We waited anxiously for the time to escape. As an alternative plan, while we were awaiting notification by Mrs. Dalton, my brother worked on a scheme to escape through the side entrance of the camp.

The camp had two entrances facing the main street. One was for the Nazis and their friends; the other side entrance was for supplies coming into the camp. The supply entrance was always locked and opened only when needed. The gate was chained and padlocked. The last time the watchman used the padlock it was jammed. He brought the padlock to be repaired at the mechanics' shop where my brother worked. While fixing the lock, he made an impression of the key by pressing it into a lump of squeezed bread and created a duplicate key. To check if the duplicate key worked, we had to try it on the real lock.

The chance came when the guard asked my brother to assist him in clearing the snow at the gate and gave him the key to open the gate for a supply wagon to pass through. My brother tried his own key, and it worked. Now we had another plan. Should the first plan with the front gate not materialize, we would try to escape through the side gate.

It was a dreary Thursday, the skies were overcast and a slight snow was starting to fall on our last day in camp. My father was at his carpenter's shop when a young man came in and told him that Misha had just left through the front gate. We had been double-crossed. The arrangements were made and my father was never told about them. Of course my father was very upset.

He came to my brother's workshop and told him what had happened. We all felt betrayed. Before we had a chance to discuss it with Mrs. Dalton, a friend of my father came into the workshop and said anyone willing to risk it could escape now because the watchman had left his tower. It was a split-second decision. My brother Osher and I were to assist my brother Paul to escape. Osher placed himself at one end of the front of the camp, and my father watched the other end. Paul, with decisive steps, approached the side gate, unlocked it, opened the gate slightly, and left the camp. I was behind him, ready to lock the gate. As I turned my head to see what was going on behind me, my father was by my side urging me to leave too. I followed my brother. I heard the click as my father locked the gate behind us.

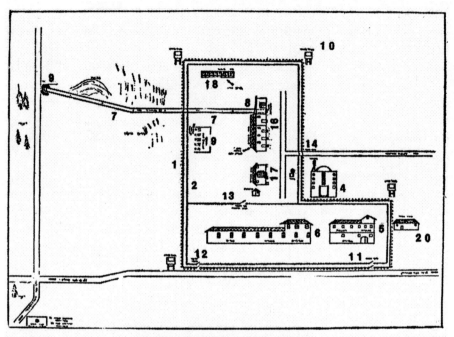

Labor Camp (Arbeitslager) Nowogrodek
Layout of the camp and tunnel

1.Barbed wire fence   2.Wooden fence   4.Former court house
5.Camp offices leather strap shop,sewing rooms
6.Shoe shop,machine shop,carpentry shop,tailor shop
7.Tunnel   8.Tunnel entrance   9.Tunnel exit 10.Watch tower
11.Main entrance to offices 12.Loading and unloading gate
13.Passage to workshops 14.Main gate   16.Barracks-Living Quarters
17.Barracks-Living Quarters 18 Toilets(Outhouse) 19.Graveyard 20.Guardhouse

It was a harsh winter in 1943 with more snow than usual. To keep the entrance to the gate clear, the snow was shoveled to both sides of the road, creating two high piles on each side of the entrance, just like a snow tunnel. While we were standing at the gate, no one from either side could see us. It was a split-second decision with split-second timing. We were sure someone above must have been watching over us. In the end, we were the only ones to escape the camp in this fashion.

As soon as we left the camp, we headed east toward the nearest forest. The highway was full of farmers coming and going to town. We even came across some German gendarmes. The weather was cold, and it was snowing, so we pulled our hats over our eyes and raised our coat collars so as to have as little face as possible visible to the outside. We continued our brisk walk until we reached the forest. When we were about 1 1/2 kilometers from camp, we dared to look back for the first time. No one was following us. We were finally free.

Even though many obstacles were still ahead of us, the feeling of freedom was exhilarating. We were not going to be led like sheep to the slaughter. Out here in the open we were free and had a fighting chance.

We took the nearest trail to the forest. The snow was well packed; the path was narrow but firm. We could hear the sound of our own footsteps. We were losing sight of the highway and getting deeper into the forest.

My brother Paul and I now decided to take a break, rest for a while, and contemplate our next move. We looked around us and saw a short row of small bushes, that would make a good hiding place should some stranger pass by through the forest. We quickly dashed into the bushes, flattened the snow into a seat, and in hushed voices discussed our next move. As we were talking, knowing that no one had seen us, we heard a voice coming across another row of bushes calling my brother's name. We were startled because it sounded like a voice from nowhere, yet it was distinctly calling Paul's name. It was like a voice from heaven. Before we had time to investigate, right across from us in the next row of bushes we saw a man stand up, and who should it be but our friend Misha who had left the camp early in the morning. We couldn't believe our eyes.

In spite of the earlier betrayal, we were glad to see a familiar face. Now we were three, and there is strength in numbers. Misha joined us and told us what had happened to him. As arranged by his mother, he left camp through the front gate. The guard at the gate was paid off, and he looked the other way. Misha was now supposed to meet with Jarmolowitz, who was waiting for him on a corner of a certain street with a horse and sleigh to take him to his farm.

In the excitement of being out and free, Misha could not find the farmer. He looked into a couple of side streets, but could find him nowhere. Afraid some passerby would recognize him and turn him into the Gestapo. Misha decided to leave town and go to the nearest forest. He was going to wait until morning and then return to camp with one of the work gangs who were led out every morning under guard to fetch water at the well. There was no running water in the labor camp.

Instead the three of us decided to continue on and try to reach the Jarmolowitz farm. We had never been there, but we had a general description and direction we should walk to reach its village.

Jarmolowitz had waited a long time but disappointedly rode back by himself to his farm when Misha did not show. Jarmolowitz was restless, and rightfully so. He knew that Misha had left the camp. If he fell into the hands of the local police or Gestapo, under torture he would eventually lead them to the farm. He warned the Jews in the bunker to be alert for any eventuality. He then went to bed, but was unable to sleep. He kept his ears tuned for any indication of trouble.

Now I must say truth is sometimes stranger than fiction. Imagine from the thousands of possibilities that Misha and we, by coincidence, should wind up sitting only a few feet away from each other in a strange forest. Again, I believe someone up there was watching over us.

The snow was getting heavier, as we started out on our way to find the farm. Originally we planned to follow the edge of the forest and continue in a westerly direction until we reached the railroad tracks, avoiding the city. As we started our march, we soon realized we could not continue in this fashion. The snow at the edge of the forest was waist deep and we weren't making much headway.

We therefore crossed an open field, coming closer to the railroad tracks we had been using as our guide. It started snowing harder and we found ourselves in the midst of a full-fledged snowstorm. Travel was difficult and Misha was becoming tired and discouraged. At one point, he picked out the nearest tree, sat under it, and refused to continue on. He was resigned to dying and could not stand any more suffering.

Paul and I tried to convince him that we had a good chance to make it and that, if he did not like the bunker, he could always join the underground and fight the Nazis. It was no use. Misha refused to budge. He urged us to leave him and go on. We explained to him that we could not leave him because our lives now were all tied together. Should the Gestapo catch him, our lives in the bunker would not be safe any more. Once they found him, how long would it take for them to catch up with us?

We were also very tired and, after arguing with Misha for a while, we compromised, we decided to go to the nearest farmhouse, pretend that we were from the Polish underground, and wait out the storm there. Misha agreed. We made him our spokesman, since he spoke a flawless Polish while my brother and I, would be recognized as Jews because of our accents. It was not safe to parade in the open as Jews, even as members of the underground.

We picked the nearest house at random and knocked on the door. The farmer let us in. Misha told him that we were members of the Polish underground and wanted to dry out and wait out the snowstorm in the house. The farmer did not object. He offered us food and a warm place near his fireplace to dry our clothing, especially our shoes and socks. We left him our socks in exchange for dry rags, which we wound around our feet to keep us dry and warm. After we ate, he asked us how long we intended to stay in his house? A new law required each farmer to notify the local police if he was going to have overnight guests. We assured him that we had no intention of staying with him overnight. As soon as it got darker, we would leave and continue on our way.

In the meantime we asked him for different directions, naming a few villages further away than the one we were heading for. He pointed the direction out to us, but warned us of the German guards who were posted at the railroad bridge we had to cross in order to get to our destination. True to our promise, as soon as it got dark, we dressed, thanked him for his hospitality, and left.

While we were leaving the farmer's house, which by local standards was poor, we envied him. He was poor but safe, tied to his native ground, and did not have to run from the Germans or the Russians, while we, the former well-to-do city dwellers, had to run for our lives.

As we stepped outside, we realized that the weather had worsened. The snowstorm had turned into a full-blown blizzard. Walking was difficult; the snowdrifts were waist high. We had no choice but to continue our march on the railroad tracks. This route was more hazardous, since the German army had stationed guards all along the railway. Our hope was that the bad weather would keep them inside their guardhouses. The wind and the cold temperature were unbearable. Even the watchdogs were in their doghouses.

We marched in a single file. Paul was at the head of the column, Misha was second and I was last. We kept a distance from each other with the understanding that should something unforeseen happen to one of us, the other two would have time to run and save themselves. It took us till midnight to reach the railroad bridge. Despite its severity, the bad weather was a blessing, keeping the Germans inside their guardhouses. As we came closer to the bridge, a light went on in a nearby farmhouse. We jumped to the side of the railroad tracks and waited. We were amazed how much light a single candle can create in total darkness. In a few minutes, the light went out.

It was time to cross the bridge. Paul went first, while Misha and I waited for an all-clear signal. As soon as all of us were across, we headed to the nearest forest and waited for a while to make sure that no one had seen us. We were now only two kilometers from our destination with one more small bridge, over a water drainage ravine to cross. From there we had to turn right into the village of Kuscino.

It was about two in the morning when we reached a little hill with some tall trees on top. We were looking for a house but could not see it.

Again we faced a dilemma. How do you find a house you have never seen? In a place you have never been to before? In total darkness? With no signs or numbers? We decided to find any house, waken the farmer, pretend that we were Russian partisans, and ask for food and directions.

Misha approached the first house we came to, knocked on the door, and ordered the door to be opened. Paul took a stick of wood from the fence surrounding the house and put it across his shoulder in the form of a gun. The farmer was slow to react to our first knock. We knocked again, more forcefully, and asked him to open the door. Finally a light went on in the house. We heard the door being unlocked and a woman in a long nightgown answered, begging us not to shoot. She claimed that they were poor farmers with no cattle to give away. We told her that we were not interested in their cattle but only in the cattle of the rich farmers, and we asked who the rich farmers were in the village. She named many of them, but the name Jarmolowitz did not come up.

In the meantime, her husband joined her and gave us a round loaf of bread. We assured him that we were not going to take his horse or cattle as long as he told us who the rich farmers were and where to find their houses. He again named a few more names, and then said there was one rich farmer living by himself whose name was Jarmolowitz. Our eyes must have popped open. Thank goodness it was dark or they would have noticed our special interest.

We asked about names they had mentioned, and directions to their farms. We took special notice when the name of Jarmolowitz was mentioned again. To our astonishment, the direction he pointed to was the top of the hill, to what we had thought was a forest. We thanked him for his kindness and left.

We headed straight to the forest and, after crossing a couple of rows of trees, we saw a house. It sat all by itself, surrounded by tall trees. In total darkness, not knowing our way, we would never have found it. Misha knew the farmer had a watchdog that by now should have barked to alert the farmer of our presence. We had been forewarned that Jarmolowitz had a tenant farmer who could not be trusted and that we should avoid alerting the members of his household.

We approached the Jarmolowitz house. There was the doghouse, but the dog refused to come out. The wind and snow kept him inside. We needed him to bark to signal Jarmolowitz of our arrival so we made snowballs and started throwing them at the doghouse. Finally the dog came out and started to bark.

As it was, Jarmolowitz had been up all night worried about Misha. When he heard the barking, he dressed and came out to see the cause of the commotion. Misha recognized him and called out his name. Jarmolowitz was relieved to see him, but was very surprised to see three of us when he had only expected one. Anyway, it was a load off his shoulders to know Misha was safe. He ordered the dog back into the doghouse and told us to follow him toward the barn. We went behind the barn in front of a cellar opening. He unlatched the padlock, opened the door and told us to follow him down into the cellar.

At that moment, many thoughts came to my mind. We had all heard stories about farmers sheltering Jews who, upon learning of the amount of gold in their possession, killed them and stole their money. Or even worse, they took your money in a facade of accepting payment for a place to hide and then turned you in to the local Gestapo. Still, we walked down the stairs in total darkness.

Once we reached the lower steps, we heard and smelled the presence of pigs. We soon learned, Jarmolowitz kept the pigs in the basement to hide them from the Germans, who were confiscating all farm animals to feed their Army. The pigsty was also used as an outhouse for the Jews hiding in the bunker. Jarmolowitz lit a match to see if all of us were with him. We were all standing at the bottom of the basement, facing the pigsty. We were told to turn around, stay away from the last three steps, and wait.

We heard him knock three times against the steps and cough once or twice. Slowly the last three steps started to move forward and to the side of where we were standing, exposing an opening in the wall. A small gas lamp appeared in an opening right behind where the steps had been. A face appeared in the opening. It was a man's face with a big mustache. It was Benson.

He motioned to us to come down into the opening. Misha was the first to put his head into the opening. Before Benson had time to tell him to lower himself feet first, he had wedged himself into the opening. We were unable to pull him back, so we had to push him in, and he landed on his face. Luckily the ground was soft and he was not hurt. I lowered myself feet first into the opening, and wound up standing on soft ground in a tunnel big enough for one person to crawl in, or walk bent over. The tunnel was about 10 feet long, supported by wooden logs overhead and on both sides. After the tunnel, we reached the main bunker and what was to be our home for the next 18 months.

The bunker was 10 feet by 8 feet wide and 6 feet high. The overhead support logs made the ceiling even lower, forcing us to lower our heads when we stood up. On the west and north sides were double wooden bunks. Benson and his wife shared one bunk. His friend, Joselewitz, had the bunk above them. Misha and Paul shared the other bunk, and I slept above them. A small wooden table took up the middle of the bunker with a small gas lamp we used only during mealtime. The rest of the time was spent in darkness except for a little airshaft not larger than the narrow side of a brick which let some dim light filter in. With the airshaft, we could separate day and night. The air duct was about six feet long. The opening at the rear of the barn was hidden from sight in the tall grass.

Our very first day in the bunker, Jarmolowitz came down to speak with the three of us. He questioned us in detail about the route we had taken to reach his farm. He feared one of the farmers had followed us to his place. We retraced our steps for him and he went back to the village to double-check our story. There he told other villagers that during the night he had been visited by bandits who took some of his grain, searched his house, and left. A villager told him that he also had visitors, partisans who came and took some of his bread and threatened to take his cow. While this confirmed our story, Jarmolowitz wanted to be certain no clue remained. He followed our footsteps and found a track of steps leading to his house through the middle of his fields. To cover our footsteps, he sent his maid, Magdalena, to walk back to the village through the field and erase our steps in the snow.

Life in the bunker was like being in a prison. The only difference being that you know the length of your sentence in prison and can count the days until your release. Our sentence had no time limit. We did not know how long we would have to stay in the bunker. The German armies were still deep within Russian territory. While their defeat at Stalingrad *(December 1942)* was a turning point in the war, it was still far away from Nowogrodek.

Jarmolowitz himself believed the Russian armies would advance in the coming spring and liberate us. This gave us the strength to endure the hardship of the bunker.

Life in the bunker became routine. We ate twice a day. The feeding time coincided with the feeding of the pigs. Magdalena had two identical pails. One was a mixture of food for the pigs, and the second pail was for us. It was a good way to disguise our food delivery in case someone noticed her going twice daily to the basement with two pails.

Mr. Benson was in charge. He had the responsibility of assigning the bunks and portioning the food. Our morning meal consisted of milk and a piece of black bread. Our afternoon meal was barley soup, another piece of bread and cooked potatoes. We seldom had any meat.

The shortage of water was another problem. While we had enough water to drink, there was not enough to wash ourselves. Every drop of water was conserved. The water we used in the morning to wash our hands and face was saved and used again to wash our underwear. We still wore the same underwear we had left the camp with. After a while white turned into gray. To dry our underwear, we used the haystack in the barn, laying it on the hay overnight to dry. Needless to say, our sanitary conditions left much to be desired.

As time passed, our food situation also became worse. Six were now sharing the same loaf of bread that originally was shared by three people. The bread was home-baked by Mrs. Jarmolowitz and she could not increase the frequency of baking lest it arouse the suspicion of the tenant farmer. We had more potatoes and milk, but that was no substitute for bread. The waiting between the morning meal and evening meal seemed endless. While we were not starving, it was nevertheless a starvation diet. We were all losing weight. Time dragged on and food was uppermost on our minds. However, our will to survive kept us going despite the depression and bleakness of our lives in the bunker.

For the first two months, the bunker was completely sealed except for the tunnel to the pigsty. The pigsty was our outhouse. The pigs thrived on human waste, growing fat while we grew thinner in the bunker.

The bunker also had another opening, which was now completely closed off. The opening led to the barn and at times was kept open to allow more air to flow in.

The Germans from time to time conducted searches to try to find hidden Jews and also to combat the partisans. The opening to the barn was not safe because a search party with dogs could easily find it. One time, after a search party had left, we came out into the barn.

It was the first time we have left the bunker in two months. It was also the first time in two months that we could see each other. The sight was not pleasant. We all had lost a lot of weight; our clothing was filthy and covered with lice, and our hair overgrown.

Life in the bunker did not appeal to us. Now that it was spring, Paul and I gave serious thought to leaving and joining the underground. We had cousins who were well established in the underground and we wished to join them. We told Benson our plan, he objected strongly. Should the Germans catch us, he feared we would be tortured until we disclosed our hiding place. Paul and Benson fell into a heated argument, whereupon Benson struck my brother. He later apologized to him.

Benson suggested we should write to our father, who was still in the camp, for advice. We agreed and wrote a letter explaining that we wished to leave the bunker for the underground. His reply was very discouraging. First he informed us that three of our cousins had been killed while fighting in the underground. Second, our youngest brother Osher was still waiting for a chance to leave the camp and join us in the bunker. He advised us to stay in the bunker. The news from the front was more encouraging and he hoped our stay would not have to continue much longer. We agreed to stay in the bunker and try to make the best of it.

From time to time we corresponded with the camp and the underground. Jarmolowitz acted as courier to deliver and receive mail from the camp to the underground. A few times, the partisans stayed in his house. They knew that he was helping us to hide, but they did not know the exact location of our bunker. Once they requested proof that we were still alive. We prepared a letter for Jarmolowitz to give to the underground assuring them that we were alive and well and asking them to ensure Jarmolowitz's protection in every way possible. Our survival was now tied to his survival.

Misha still had his parents in the camp, and we had our brother and father. Should they manage to escape, we knew that the bunker could not hold all of us and planned that some of us should join the underground if space became limited.

Little did we know we would still be in the bunker when the German search & destroy ended in the spring of 1943. It was decided to unseal the opening from the bunker to the barn. We established a 24-hour watch to guard the entrance to the bunker. The guard was always on the lookout for any sign that our hiding place might be discovered. In the daytime only one guard was required, but at night we had teams of two. Should one fall asleep, the other would be there to wake him.

Only Tina, Benson's wife, was excused from guard duty. Positioning the guards at the south side of the barn wall gave us a complete view of the two houses and the entire farmyard between them. At night we relied on Jarmolowitz's dog for early detection of anyone suspicious. His barking would give us time to enter the bunker and conceal the entrance.

Being discovered by strangers was not our only fear; we also had to keep ourselves hidden from Jarmolowitz's two young granddaughters. The children, (ages 4 and 5-1/2), were very active, roaming the farm freely and often making their way into the barn. We were very careful not to expose ourselves to them realizing, that as children, they could not understand the necessity of keeping our hiding place a secret.

One spring day, Benson decided to get some fresh air. He left the bunker for the barn and spread himself out on the top of the haystack to enjoy the sweet smell of the fresh cut grass and fell asleep. The children in their playful way made a dash toward the barn. Joselevitz had enough time to go down into the bunker and cover the entrance. Benson was left sleeping on the haystack.

Jolanta looked for a place to hide. She run up the haystack and found Benson. Frightened, she ran to her grandfather, telling him that she had seen a strange man in the barn. As she left the barn, Benson awakened and signaled to be admitted into the bunker by tapping three times at the opening. He came down into the bunker concerned about what would happen next.

As we expected, Jarmolowitz arrived shortly thereafter complaining that our carelessness was endangering his life and the life of his entire family. How do you explain a strange man to a five-year-old child? He could not admit to her that there was a man in the barn lest she repeat the story to strangers. He devised a story, taking an old fur coat, which farmers sometimes put on top of a haystack to air out, putting it in the same spot where Benson had been sleeping. He told Jolanta that all she had seen was a coat and not a man as she thought. When Jolanta returned to the haystack with her grandfather and saw the old coat, she was skeptical but accepted her grandfather's explanation.

This incident made us realize how serious was the threat of an accidental discovery. We came to understand that regardless of our carefulness, something unforeseen could happen.

It was time to discuss what to do in the event one of us was caught outside the bunker. We agreed that, in such an emergency, we would wait until midnight for that captured party's return. If no one returns the bunker would be abandoned that night.

We hoped that we would never be forced to use this plan, but what had happened with Jolanta convinced us that we must have agreed-upon arrangements.

As it happened, at a later time we did come very close to having to abandon the bunker.

8

BIELSKI'S PARTISANS

Since the German defeat at Stalingrad the Russian underground became more menacing. At night they controlled most of the villages in and around our area. They blew up the railroad bridges, and cut the telephone wires, becoming a threat to the German hinterland. From time to time the German army with the help of the local collaborators would comb the nearby forest and farms. Most of the time they came up empty-handed.

The Partisans were an elusive group that moved quickly from forest to forest. Their main base of operation was located in the forest of Naliboki. They had their contacts in the local villages who kept them informed on the movements of the German army and their collaborators. When the German Army came closer to our village, we decided that it was time again to block the entrance to our bunker in the barn. We removed the box filled with earth and the retaining walls around it. The entrance was filled with earth that we leveled off to match the floor of the barn. We didn't have to wait long. After a couple of days the German Army came to our village. We could hear the dogs barking as they approached the farm. The Nazis used bloodhounds in their search for hidden Jews or Partisans. As the barking got louder we could hear them come into the stable. We heard the voices of their handlers. Luckily they didn't detect anything and soon left the ranch. Being sealed in the bunker was very confining. The only exit left open for us was the tunnel leading to the pigsty, which we used as an outhouse. After some time, when we were sure that the search and destroy action was over, we again unearthed and opened the entrance from the bunker to the barn.

One of our most loyal and trusted friends was the dog Jarmolovitz had on his ranch. By nature it hated military men. The dog could smell an armed person approaching the farm from miles away. Every time the dog started to bark, we knew that we had to take cover. At night the dog was our eyes and ears. He never failed to warn us of approaching danger.

I remember one night, when we had a visit from a group of armed Russian partisans; the dog wouldn't stop barking. The Partisan group entered the Jarmolowitz house, leaving one man to guard the front yard. The barking of the dog so annoyed the Partisan that he took out a knife and stabbed the dog. In the morning when we found out what happened we were saddened by the thought that we had lost our best friend. Luckily the dog survived and recovered. The dog was the unsung hero of our survival.

The Partisans continued to menace the German hinterland. Their method of operation was to avoid engaging the German army in open warfare. The Partisans picked the time and place of attack. Their main mission was to blow up bridges, railroad tracks, and telephone poles and to raid small German units.

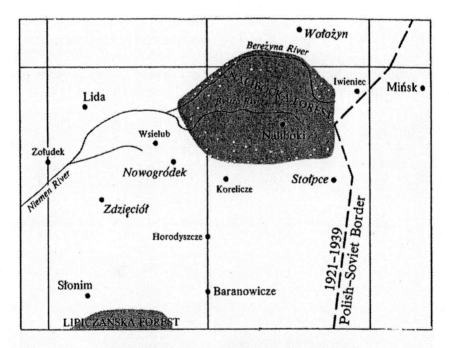

North Eastern part of prewar Poland
Nowogrodek and surrounding towns
And villages. Forest of Naliboki

As I mentioned before, the Partisan main base of operation was located in the forest of Naliboki. There they had their central command that controlled all the Partisan groups in our area. Most of their units consisted of fighting men only. One of the groups, which accepted women and children, was a Jewish Partisan group organized by the Bielski brothers.

The Bielski brothers lived in the small village of Stankiewitz. After the ghetto of Nowogrodek was established the Jewish families still living in the nearby villages were ordered to move into the ghetto. Most of the families complied except for the Bielski brothers who chose to live in the nearby forest. This was the beginning of the Bielski Partisan group.

After the second mass killing of the Jews in Nowogrodek, more of the surviving young Jews left the ghetto and joined up with the Bielski group. Among them were my cousin Yehoshua Abramovitz and our second cousins, the Polonski brothers. From time to time the Jewish partisans slipped into the ghetto urging more young Jews to join them in the underground. At that time, many arguments ensued among the elders of the ghetto and the young men. The elders were clinging to the so-called security of the ghetto with the illusion that the Germans might spare them, while the younger men were willing to take chances by joining up with the Partisans and fighting the Nazis. Our elders who were tamed city dwellers could not envision life without the protection of a roof over their heads. They agreed that in the summer time we would survive in the open, but come winter we would perish. Their argument convinced many of the younger generation to stay in the Ghetto.

My cousins, Abramovitz and Polonskis were excellent fighters. In the Bielski group they were heralded as heroic soldiers. They fought the Germans and their collaborators, taking revenge for the death of their mothers, fathers, brothers and sisters.

On one of their successful missions to obtain provisions, our cousins, part of a select group of 10 Jewish Partisans stopped to rest at a farmer's house. The farmers place was considered a safe house for Partisans. They drank a toast with the farmer and went to sleep. One man was posted to guard the house. While the Partisans were sleeping one of the farmers sons sneaked out the house and ran into the city of Nowogrodek to inform the Gestapo that Jewish Partisans were sleeping in his father's house. His motive was money. The German authorities offered fifty marks for capturing a Jew or a Partisan. The Gestapo with a company of German soldiers quietly came to the village, surrounded the farmer's house and, without a fight captured the Jewish Partisans. The only survivor was the guard who ran into the forest to avoid capture. My cousins and their Partisan friends were all killed.

The news of the partisans' capture and killing spread to all surrounding villages. The mood in the Bielski Group was somber. Not only did they lose good combatants, but also the action of the farmer's son threatened the safety of all other Partisan Groups. It was decided to take revenge. They waited a couple of weeks for the environment to calm down. After the cooling off period, they asked for volunteers to take part in the revenge action. The best of the fighting men volunteered for the incursion.

On a quiet night the Jewish Partisans entered the village. After securing all the roads to the village, they marched to the farmer's house. The Partisan fighters surrounded the house. The house and the barns were torched with all the family members inside. Anyone trying to escape was gunned down. On the same night other Partisan groups went to the farmer's aunts and uncles and burned their homes. After this action proclamations were posted all over the villages informing the farmers that betrayal of any Partisan is punishable by death. From that day on it became safer for a Partisan or a Jew to enter a farmer's house and walk freely in the villages. This episode taught us the lesson to fight terror with terror. This was the only language the Gestapo and their collaborating farmers respected.

9

JAN AND JOSEFA JARMOLOWITZ

Wacek Jarmolowitz killed by Nazis

The life of Jan Jarmolowitz was intertwined with the existence of Poland. Born in the late 1880's, Jarmolowitz joined Pilsudski's legionnaires in 1920 to fight the Russians. After the treaty of Brest-Litowsk, Poland gained more territory in the east. As a reward the legionnaires who helped Pilsudski were given free land in the eastern territories. Jarmolowitz, for his service with the Polish Legion, was given free land and a house in the village of Kuscino.

The farm in Kuscino
Location of the houses and barn not to scale
The hideout bunker was located under the barn

The majority of farmers in the village were Byelorussian. The newcomers were called "Osadnik", *(Polish for settlers)*. After settling in Kuscino, Jan Jarmolowitz was married to Josefa. She soon bore him a son, Wacek. Jarmolowitz built himself a new house, renting his old house to a tenant farmer who helped him with his farm work in return for a share of the crops. As he no longer had to attend to his farm, Jarmolowitz pursued business in the city of Nowogrodek.

By profession Jarmolowitz was a butcher, having learned to make Polish sausage in his youth. He rented a shop in the marketplace in Nowogrodek and opened a butcher store. Jarmolowitz used part of his farm to raise pigs, which he later slaughtered and sold in his shop. Business was good and, as a farmer and a businessman, Jarmolowitz soon became well-to-do. He traveled extensively to Wilno and Warsaw, where he made business contacts to sell more meat products. He became reacquainted with many of his old-time friends, many of whom, because of their service in the war, were now high officials in the Polish government.

Poland under Pilsudski was prosperous, and so was Jarmolowitz. After the death of Pilsudski *(1935)*, Poland took a definite turn to the right. Nazism and anti-Semitism were crossing the border from Germany into Poland. A new Polish organization was formed in Nazi style called *"Mloda Polska"* Young Poland. Mloda Polska had core groups in every town and village in Poland. They organized boycotts of Jewish businesses and urged farmers not to deal with the Jews. One of their plans was to drive the Jews out of business by establishing competing Christian-owned stores. However, the Christian stores met with little success, since their prices were higher and the farmers shopped where they could get the best deal.

Not able to compete with the Jewish-owned businesses, Mloda Polska started to harass some of the Jewish-owned stores, breaking display windows and inflicting damage by breaking displayed pottery. The young among the Jews organized a self-defense group. They knew who the perpetrators were and one evening invited them for a drink. While they were drinking, the defense group arrived and warned them to stop harassing the Jews. The offenders were severely beaten and the defense group promised them more of the same if they did not stop the harassment of the Jews.

It was rumored that Wacek, while not personally involved, supported the members of the "Mloda Polska". This indicated where the sympathies of the Jarmolowitz family were at this time, nationalistic and right wing.

After Hitler's attack on Poland in September 1939 and the collapse of the Polish Army, the Russians crossed the Polish border and took control of the so-called "abandoned" eastern territories of Poland. Jarmolowitz now had to make the crucial decision of either staying in Nowogrodek and face the Russians or cross over into the western part of Poland to avoid a confrontation with his old enemies, the Bolsheviks. Jarmolowitz and his son decided to cross over into Western Poland, out of reach of the Russians. They left their families behind, hoping the women would not be mistreated. Their whereabouts and activities in Western Poland are unknown to me.

Poland was now divided into two halves, one controlled by the Germans and the other by the Russians. For the women of the Jarmolowitz household, events took a turn for the worse. Mrs. Jarmolowitz, her daughter-in-law, two granddaughters, and their maid, Magdalena, were ordered to leave their big house and move into the smaller quarters, which previously had housed their tenant farmer. The poor tenant farmer moved into the big house.

With no men around to support them, life for the Jarmolowitz family got worse. The women were forced to sell some of their possessions to survive. They lived with the constant fear of being exiled to Siberia.

As time went on, the Russians instigated a drive to incorporate the territories they called Western Byelorussia into the Republic of Byelorussia. A committee was formed from the local population, which petitioned Stalin for acceptance into the Russian Empire. The territories were accepted into the Byelorussian Republic. Elections were held to elect representatives to the National Assembly. The candidates were hand-picked by the Communist Party from the local population. The election was compulsory, and 99% of the people voted for the candidates, since no opposition was allowed. The entire population became Russian citizens, part of mother Russia.

The Polish schools were abolished and a new Russian school system was established under the watchful eye of the Communist Party. Principals and teachers were shipped in from the east to supervise the Communist indoctrination of the young.

In school I was introduced to the theoretical idea of Communism, which sounded fine, but I soon found out it did not work in practical terms. While all men are created equal it is there that the similarity ends. Each person has different abilities and different needs. Despite the inconsistencies, the changes showed us the Russians were here to stay.

After the integration of the Polish territory into the Republic of Byelorussia, life returned to normal for most of the local population except for the formerly rich and those who had been part of the Polish government. Mrs. Jarmolowitz was concerned because, not only had they been considered well-to-do, they had close ties with the former Polish leaders, and their husbands were on the other side of the border in German-occupied Poland.

As the months passed, Wacek's wife, Jadviga, ventured out from their small village of Kuscino to visit the city of Nowogrodek. Jadviga was a comely woman, blond with blue eyes and a well-proportioned figure.

The local head of the NKVD *(Soviet secret police)* noticed her good looks. She was without a husband, and he had been away from his wife for many months. They found consolation in each other's company. Jadviga visited the city more often and was able to get additional food and goods, which had become scarce since the Communists took over. She was lonely and may have been tempted by the Russian's good looks. However, another member of the NKVD picked her up one night, she was trapped. He accused her on trumped up political charges. She was arrested and later exiled to Siberia.

The Jarmolowitz's whole world was crumbling. Jadviga's children were now without a mother or father. The hardships they had endured were now compounded by the fear of exile for the entire family. Jadviga was taken by horse-driven wagon to the railroad station in Novojelna. There she was put in a railroad car with other families being exiled to Siberia.

Many of the families being exiled were former members of the Polish police or former high officials of the Polish government. Also included among the exiles were some Jewish families who, because of their prior wealth, were now being sentenced to Siberia. The men and women were separated, the men being kept under heavy guard to prevent their escape.

This was the summer of 1941, when the Western press predicted an imminent attack on Russia by the German Army. Instead of fortifying the border with Germany, the Russians were busy transporting the exiles to Siberia. By the time the train reached the city of Minsk, the German Army attacked a wide sector of the Russian border. The Germans bombed the border towns, creating panic among the civilian population. The German "Blitzkrieg" had begun. The Russian Army was retreating in panic, leaving behind all their tanks and planes.

The exiles found out about the war while they were still on their way to Siberia. War did not stop the trains, which continued eastward until they reached their Siberian destination. In Siberia, Jadviga was assigned to a brigade of women to clean the barracks in preparation for the arrival of more exiles from the western territories. However, the German attack on Russia stopped the flow of exiles and, after Stalin allied himself with the Western powers at the end of 1941, all former Polish citizens were released from the custody of the NKVD.

Unfortunately, because of the war and the German occupation of the western territories of Russia, the freed exiles could not return home. Most of those released settled in nearby communal "Kolhoz" *(collective farms)* to wait out the war.

After the defeat of the German Army, most of those who survived the ordeal of Siberia returned home. It was more than three years after her exile that Jadviga was able to return home to her children, and to the rest of the family.

She was unprepared for the tragic events that had befallen her family during the German occupation of Poland and Russia.

With the initial German victory over Russia, Jan and Wacek Jarmolowitz returned to their home in the village of Kuscino. Overjoyed to be home again, they were thankful to the German Army for making their return possible. They joined a group of ethnic Germans, former citizens of Poland who were returning home to Nowogrodek. Among them was Wacek's friend Fulda. Fulda was a former Polish citizen of German descent. Unknown to Wacek, Fulda was also a secret member of the SS who would be called to help administer his former hometown. The reunion of Jan and Wacek Jarmolowitz with their families was tearful and sad. The joy of seeing their families again was marred because Jadviga was not there. There was nothing the Jarmolowitz's could do then to locate her. Only a total German victory might hasten her return. Wacek became aware of rumors concerning his wife's arrest but decided to reserve judgment until she returned home and could provide an explanation. He was glad to see his two beautiful children. They gave him a lot of comfort in what was for him a very trying time.

Upon his return, Wacek went to Nowogrodek for a reunion with all of his former Polish friends. After all, he was Polish and a patriot. Why not use the German victory for the benefit of Poland and establish a new Polish administration in Nowogrodek? A committee of 50 Polish men was formed to discuss its ideas with the local German authorities. The idea was for an anti-Russian Poland friendly to Germany. They believed that the German authorities would be sympathetic to this idea. Unknown to Wacek and his friends, the Germans had their own ideas about governing the occupied territories.

The Germans considered the territories as occupied Byelorussian land and not Polish land. They intended to administer the territories themselves.

Desiring no opposition or competition, they notified the Polish group not to create any kind of administration or engage in any form of self-government. Germany would govern, and Germany would assign the new administration. Ignoring the German edict, the Polish group had a meeting where it was decided not to conform to the German wishes but to form a de-facto Polish administration.

This was the summer of 1941, when on a Saturday 50 Jews were executed in the market place by the Nazis. The whole town was stunned by the tragedy.

The murderous act was discussed at the next meeting of the Polish group, where the Jews suffered criticism for not resisting the Germans.

A few weeks later, the same Polish group was invited to meet with the commandant of the local Gestapo to discuss the formation of their self-government. To their surprise and disbelief, they were all arrested and taken to the local prison house. Early the next morning they were taken by truck outside the city and killed by firing squad at the forest of Skridleve for disobeying the German order against organizing a Polish self-government. Some of the local farmers were called to assist the Gestapo to bury them in a mass grave. The next morning, official proclamations were posted all over town notifying the local residents of the execution of the Polish patriots as a warning to the local population that disobedience of a German order meant death.

Among those killed at the forest of Skridleve was Wacek Jarmolowitz, son of Jan Jarmolowitz. Previously, the Russians had arrested Jan Jarmolowitz's daughter-in-law, exiling her to Siberia and depriving their grandchildren of a mother. Now the Germans had killed their father. While there was hope for the return of their mother once the war ended, their father, a victim of Nazi brutality, would never return. Jan Jarmolowitz now turned his hatred of Russia against the Germans and their cohorts. Outwardly he still professed his previously anti-Bolshevik views, but inwardly he looked for ways to fight and defeat the Nazis.

Since Hitler's intent was to kill all the Jews in Nowogrodek and the surrounding area, Jarmolowitz vowed to thwart the Nazi purpose by saving the Jews.

On his next trip to visit the workshop of the forced labor camp, he made contact with a Jewish family and advised them of his willingness to assist Jews. In order to survive on his farm, he needed money to sustain himself and the Jews he was going to hide.

A family friend approached my father, as it was known within the camp that he was in possession of gold and was willing to pay to save his children.

My father now looked for ways for us to escape from the forced labor camp, since Jarmolowitz agreed to keep us hidden for the duration of the war.

10

FOURTH MASS MURDER— MAY 7, 1943 OSHER KILLED MASS ESCAPE FROM CAMP SEPTEMBER 25, 1943

From time to time we corresponded with the Labor Camp and the underground. Jarmolowitz acted as the courier with messages moving through the tailor shop, where my Uncle Chaim worked. Besides doing the required work for the German Army, the workers also made custom-made clothing, for the local Christian population, as long as they supplied their own material and thread. This contact with civilians allowed the camp to keep in touch with the outside world by sending notes in the unused materials and thread, which was always returned to the owners. We wrote our letters to the camp on an old piece of paper, crumpled them into balls, and then wound thread around the ball of paper like a spool. The thread containing our hidden messages was given to my uncle, who delivered it to my father. In the same fashion, letters were transmitted back to us in the bunker.

Many times the Partisans who still had family and friends in the camp would give Jarmolowitz letters to be taken into the camp the same way. Because the letters were written in Yiddish, Jarmolowitz would have us read and censor the letters. He didn't want information that would incriminate him revealed. One letter had a comic line, which I still remember to this day. Two Partisans with a brother-in-law in the labor camp asked him for a sign he was still alive. The letter read, "If you are alive, why is it we don't hear from you? However, if you are dead, then let us know."

Because this system went through the tailor shop, my uncle was aware of all the escape plans my father made for my youngest brother, Osher, who was still in the camp with our father. We urged them to leave the camp and join us. We expected Osher to come first, but as things turned out, we were never to see him again. Instead, Jarmolowitz told us one spring day that we had a guest. It turned out to be our cousin, Pesach.

As I learned years later, my father had arranged Osher's escape by bribing the guard at the front gate. My brother had been ready to leave but a group of tailors, including my uncle who knew my father's plans, stopped Osher from leaving by way of the tailor shop. My cousin Pesach took my brother's place. My uncle argued someone else should be given a chance to survive, since my father already had two children on the outside. My father believed the episode at the tailor shop devastated Osher. He was the youngest one, and the loss of our mother followed by our leaving the camp made him feel abandoned. The final betrayal destroyed him physically and mentally. The circumstances surrounding my brother's death remained a barrier between my uncle and my father until the end of my father's life. My father never forgave him.

The last organized slaughter, in which my brother Osher was killed, was the most gruesome killing witnessed in the camp. In prior cases, they took the people away from the camp and killed them out of the sight of the survivors. Not this time. It was May 7, 1943. We were told the day started as a normal day, but soon prisoners again experienced the atrocities inflicted by the Nazis. This time, all in the camp witnessed the killing. The Germans had established a new system of deceit. Workers were divided into two groups, one group getting the normal ration of bread and the second group getting a double portion of bread.

Then, unexpectedly, the Nazis and their henchmen surrounded the camp. The two groups were separated. The group receiving the double portion of bread was taken into the workshop. The Nazis and local Police force immediately rounded up the other group. Panic gripped all the inmates. The barracks were searched and more inmates were chased out to join the unfortunate group. Under heavy guard, the whole group of about 250 was led from camp. They were marched to open sand pits only a few hundred meters from camp. There in full view of the survivors, they were shot execution-style and thrown into the pits. Thus, fathers had to watch the killing of their children, including my brother Osher, my aunt Cypke with her three children. The Police made no effort to hide what they were doing. Farmers coming into town and workers doing their daily task saw it. The surviving Jews remember this as the fourth and final mass murder "Shechita" in Nowogrodek. Within hours, the whole spectacle was over. The remaining inmates were then forced into workshops to continue their slave labor. To many who witnessed this, including my father, life lost its meaning. Now they would rather die escaping than wait for the "Final Solution".

My father now had the sad task of writing to us of our brother's death and also of informing Misha he was now an orphan. Both of his parents, realizing that their end was near, took an overdose of sleeping pills. By the time they were taken to the slaughter, both of them were in a deep state of sleep.

Jarmolowitz brought the letter from my father, first giving it to Benson. He read the letter and told Misha, Paul, and myself to sit down and promise him that we would not cry. He then told us the bad news. We were all in shock. The first thing that came to my mind was that they tried to escape from the camp, got caught in the wires, and were killed. It did not dawn on us another killing would follow so soon after the last mass murders in February 1943. True to our promise, we did not cry. I had cried myself out when my mother was killed in August 1942. The loss of my mother before the German slaughters became commonplace was the biggest blow of my life.

Benson, in trying to console us, told us that it was now our duty to be calm and survive because our lives in the bunker were not all that safe. He compared our lives, and the lives of the partisan, to those of wild or domesticated geese. The wild goose is free to fly in search of food, but in the end could be shot and killed by a hunter. The domesticated geese are fed daily, but at any given moment can be taken to the slaughter. We are the same. Even in the safety of the bunker, one day we could be discovered and taken to the slaughter like the domesticated geese. Like the wild geese, my cousin and other partisans in the underground were free, but they had to fight for their food, and in the end, the Nazis would kill them.

With the arrival of my cousin Pesach, the food situation worsened, since we had to divide our already meager portions of food seven ways instead of six. Although the population of the bunker increased, the amount of food did not. Hunger was our constant companion. Benson and his wife were the only couple in our bunker, and Benson was in charge of rationing the food. He tried to be fair to all, but you always imagined that the next portion was larger than yours. Always alert to the possibility that our food supply might one day be cut off completely, it was decided that a food reserve should be established. Each day we saved a piece of bread until each of us had a supply to last for a couple of days.

Unexpectedly, though, this hoarding gave rise to a new problem: How to keep the mice away from our bread? The field mice had been our only companions since we begun our tenure in the bunker. We were glad to have them. We had convinced ourselves that as long as the mice did not abandon us, our bunker was safe. We had to find a way, though, to keep them away from our bread. We had no hiding place, and every imaginable place we tried, they found and nibbled on our bread.

One night we tried to hang the bread in the middle of the bunker suspended by a belt from the ceiling. For a few nights it worked. We thought we had licked the problem, but after a while the mice learned to walk across the ceiling and down the belt and again nibble on the bread.

My father was still in the camp. He and the remaining Jews finally realized they would have to escape if they wanted to survive. They knew from a secret radio receiver the war was going badly for the Germans. Sooner or later, the Germans would have to retreat. They were also certain that, even in defeat, they would kill the remaining Jews. A plan was devised to dig a tunnel from the barracks to the wheat field where the entrance to the tunnel would be camouflaged by the stalks of green. To dig an underground tunnel in secret under the nose of the German guards required the physical and material resources of the entire camp. The carpenters stole pieces of wood from their workshop, smuggled them into the barracks, and made supports to keep the earth from collapsing on the diggers. Only one person at a time could dig. To dig for just an hour required a physical dexterity and stamina that taxed the inmates' remaining reserves of strength. With determination, however, the work continued on a twenty-four hour basis. As the length of the tunnel increased, the carpenters constructed a wooden carriage on wheels to haul the dirt from the ground. The carriage ran on wooden tracks pulled by a rope around a pulley. The problem was how to dispose of the dirt? First the workers filled up the attics, and then they constructed double walls and filled them in with earth. In the summer of 1943, after months of digging, the tunnel was finished and preparations were made to escape.

Now the question arose as to who should go first? Of course, everyone wanted to be among the first to leave because it was thought, they would have a better chance of survival. Arguments ensued and fights broke out. In a matter of life and death, there were few compromises as the inmates looked for a solution.

In the meantime, the wheat in the fields was harvested and the tall grass that had hidden the opening of the tunnel was cut away. The time of the escape was delayed because it became necessary to dig further out into the field to provide coverage for the opening of the tunnel.

No one wanted to be among the last hundred inmates to leave the camp. The thought of being in the last group was both frightening and depressing. After much deliberation, the inmates finally arrived at a solution. A committee was chosen with full authority to decide the lineup, which was not to be disclosed to any of the inmates. Each inmate was given only the name of the person he or she was to follow on the night of the escape. Only the committee knew the numerical order. Arguments would not be tolerated, and anyone protesting the plan, or his position would be liquidated at once. This arrangement seemed to please everyone.

Before a solution was reached, my father, hearing the endless arguments among the camp inmates, doubted they would ever escape. He therefore decided to take a chance and try to save himself. On a nice summer's day in June 1943, my father went to the fence, opened the hole the guard used to look into the camp, crawled through the hole in the fence, made it to the barbed wires, pulled up the wires and crawled under until he caught himself, tearing his shirt and scratching his hands. He managed to make it safely across the ravine and the empty field into the forest. The way my father described it, it was a sheer miracle that no one saw him break out from camp. God must have been watching over him.

My father knew the countryside well. He made it safely to the Jarmolowitz farm in broad daylight, but stayed in hiding until evening, whereupon he approached Jarmolowitz. The farmer waited until total darkness before he led my father to us. Now we were eight.

With the arrival of my father, the food situation worsened. Now the same loaf of bread had to be cut into eight pieces. We were running short of money and hoped that my father had more gold. But, as things turned out, he had lost all the gold in the last liquidation at the camp when he turned all his money over to my brother Osher. Since we had escaped camp, my father had been in constant fear if we were discovered missing Osher would be executed as a consequence. He even went to the extent of changing my brother's identity. There was another person missing in the camp and they gave his name to my brother to make it appear as if he were a member of another family. On the day of the last liquidation at the camp, fearing our escape would be discovered, my father turned over all his gold to my brother Osher. The gold went with him to his grave.

Jarmolowitz was disappointed that my father did not bring more money. We still had American dollars, but Jarmolowitz claimed they were of no value to him since the farmers refused to accept paper money. We urged him to take our dollars and hold them until the end of the war, and then we would exchange them for gold. He reluctantly accepted all the dollars we had. His life and our lives were now tied together. The Jewish underground knew about us and from time to time requested written proof that we were still alive.

Summer was giving way to fall, and we all realized that we would have to spend another winter in the cold bunker.

Back at the camp, the 300 remaining prisoners waited to escape. On a rainy night of September 25, 1943, the inmates decided that the time had arrived. My brother and I were on guard duty that night in the barn. Learning about the construction of the tunnel from our father, we both felt that this would be an appropriate night to escape, since visibility was zero. The longer it took the Germans to detect the escape, the better the chance of the inmates' survival. However, as an additional precaution and as a signal that the escape was on, they short-circuited the searchlight on the guard's observation tower. The inmates proceeded as planned. The ground to the outside was broken open, and the first group left the camp. They were the most experienced men in handling firearms in case of a fight. The last to leave was my cousin Pejsach and his friend Idel, both crippled by frostbites. It was their job to put out the gas lamp and close the opening to the tunnel.

What happened in those final minutes is pure speculation, but the survivors of the escape assumed the gas lamp must have turned over and started a fire. When the guards saw the fire, they entered the camp to awaken the inmates, but all they found were empty bunks. Realizing there had been a mass escape they started to shoot in all directions. The group that had been the first to leave were the farthest from the camp, but when the shooting began, they became confused. In the total darkness, they made a wrong turn, heading back to the camp instead of out to the forest. The guards gunned many of them down. My crippled cousin Pejsach with his friend Idel, the last to leave the camp made it safely to the underground.

My uncle Chaim with his daughter and son came to our farm. They asked Jarmolowitz if they could join us in the bunker. We advised them in writing that the bunker could not accommodate more people. We suggested that they leave the barn and join the Bielski partisan group. We even made mention that in case of emergency we might join them in the forest. A few days after the escape, the Germans discontinued their search for the runaway Jews and closed up the Labor Camp. My uncle and cousins took our advice. They left the safety of our barn and joined the Bielski Partisan group.

It was seven critical days for five people who had decided not to join in the master plan of escape.

One sickly man with his 14-year old son and a sister with her brother and brother-in-law, all of them sick and debilitated, felt that they could not survive the rigor of escape. Rather than be in the way of the escapees they asked to be left in the camp and be sealed in a hideout they constructed in the attic near the chimney of the barrack. They prepared food and water to last them for days. When the signal was given to escape they entered the attic and were sealed from the outside.

After the escape they heard all the commotion and shooting going on in and around the camp. A few days after the big escape The Germans removed the guards and abandoned the Labor Camp. When things got quiet, they unsealed the hideout and slowly walked away from the camp. They were successful in finding the Bielski Partisans and all survived the war.

About a 170 inmates survived the escape thru the underground tunnel. It is interesting to note, that to the best of my knowledge, this was the one and only successful mass escape from a German Labor Camp in all of Byelorussia.

11

BEINES 1944

Since he joined us in hiding in the summer of 1943, my father never ventured outside the bunker. Because of his age (about 40) he was excused from guard duty. We were not sure if he had the agility or the speed needed in time of an emergency to reenter the bunker and cover the entrance. The cover to the entrance of the bunker consisted of a square box about 30 inches by 30 inches filled with earth to resemble the floor of the barn. It was pretty heavy and we were not sure if my father could handle it. But, with the arrival of spring and the good news from the Russian front, my father offered to help on night guard duty outside the bunker.

Until then the 24-hour guard myself, my brother Paul, Misha, Benson and Joselevitz, manned duty outside the bunker. We agreed that the night duty would be less dangerous for him than the daytime duty. However on one of his nights of guard duty, we came close to a disaster.

Jarmolowitz always warned us to watch out for his tenant farmer Novogran, telling us that he was not honest. During the day we always kept an eye on his movements, but at night we had to rely on our senses. Our food supplies were meager and food, or, better, the lack of it, was constantly on our mind. All of us lost weight and were on a look out for Jarmolowitz, who from time to time would drop in with an extra loaf of bread. The doors to the barn were always locked for the night, but there was enough space under the door for someone to slide under and enter the barn. This was the way Jarmolowitz would enter the barn in the late evening to bring us some food or just for a visit.

On one night of his guard duty, my father heard someone approaching the barn, and it seemed to him that the person was coming from Jarmolowitz's house. My father figured that this must be our lucky night since the man was bringing us more bread. In total darkness it was difficult to distinguish, who was approaching the barn. When he heard the man slide under the barn door, he assumed that it was Jarmolowitz.

My father walked slowly in the dark and stumbled into the incoming man. The man turned out to be taller than Jarmolowitz. He grabbed my father by the throat, and asked him in a whispering voice who he was. My father had to think fast. Realizing that the person was not Jarmolowitz, he replied in a shaky voice that he was a poor farmer who came in the barn to steal some of the ham Jarmolowitz was curing in the barn. This was the same answer he got from the stranger. They both seemed shaken. My father realized that the thief must be Novogran, the tenant farmer, who lived in the small house on Jarmolowitz's property.

After the encounter in the barn, Novogran left the same way he came in and went back to his house. My father was certain that Novogran would be waiting to see if he also left the barn. Without telling us, my father left the barn by sliding under the door, walked by the window where the tenant farmer was watching and then turned right in the direction of Jarmolowitz's house. As soon as he cleared the big house he turned again to the right to be out of everyone's view.

The commotion in the barn woke up Benson, he came out to look for my father but he was nowhere to be found. Benson came down to the bunker and woke all of us. We now faced a real emergency. We had previously discussed the possibility of such an incident, and we had made contingency plans. We had agreed that if any one of us found ourselves in a position, which might endanger the safety of the others in the bunker, after a short wait, we would all leave, escape to the nearest forest and eventually join the Partisans. We now had only a couple of hours to make a fateful decision.

My father, after a short while, headed out to the fields with the understanding, that if he did not return soon, we would abandon the bunker. To avoid being detected by Novogran who would still be watching the barn door from his window, he decided to reach the bunker by the rear entrance through the basement. But the door to the basement was locked. With his bare hands till they were bleeding my father dug a hole in the ground under one of the sides of the basement. He created a crawl space big enough for him to enter the basement. Once he was down in the basement he moved the last three steps to reveal the emergency door to the bunker. He gave the prearranged signal by knocking three times on the door. We heard his knocking on the door and waited for the second signal, which was a few coughs. Slowly we opened the entrance to see my father shaken but in one piece. All of us were glad to see him and to find out what happened. He told and retold the story of the encounter with Novogran.

It was now our time to make a judgment if anything was compromised as to the safety of the bunker. After analyzing everything my father had told us we agreed our secret location was still safe. My father had handled the situation as well as was possible under the circumstances.

The next morning we had to face Jarmolowitz and tell him what happened. He scolded us for being careless. In his fashion he reminded us that we were destined to die, but why do we have to endanger his life, and the life of his entire family? The penalty for hiding Jews meant death to all of us. Needless to say he was very upset but the situation had to be rectified.

He came up with an idea to engage Novogran in conversation and mention to him that someone stole a ham that he was curing in the barn. From the conversation with Novogran, Jarmolowitz concluded everything was safe for the time being.

12

COSSACKS

The Red Army with their summer offensive of 1943, had retaken the German occupied Cossack land in the Kuban region, north of the Caucasus. Hitler had ordered his troops to help the fleeing Cossacks. Thousands of Cossacks withdrew westward. The Germans had assigned to them as a place of settlement the district around the town of Nowogrodek. The Cossacks didn't come by themselves. They brought along their families and everything else they could load on their wagons, including household items and livestock. At Nowogrodek they hoped to sit out the war and eventually return to their land in the Kuban or Don. The local population was ordered to accommodate the Cossacks by providing them with housing. Nowogrodek became the temporary headquarters for the Cossacks self-defense force. They even published their own newspaper.

Jarmolowitz with his big house was ordered to accept a Cossack family. An enemy family living in his house created new problems for us. How do you explain the large amount of bread Mrs. Jarmolowitz had to bake, or the cooking of so many potatoes? Jarmolowitz told the Cossack family that he was raising pigs in the basement in secret, since all livestock had to be turned in to the German authorities. Our food problems namely the lack of it intensified.

We had to be on constant guard to watch out for the uninvited guests. On Sundays Jarmolowitz's house was being used as a Cossack church. Many times the Cossacks left their guns standing only a hand length away from our barn. On Sundays the barn was mostly locked, and standing guard we were able to listen in on many of their conversations. It was beginning to dawn on the Cossacks that the Germans will lose the war and that joining up with the Nazis had been a mistake.

One day Jarmolowitz told us about a Jewish family that was hiding in a nearby village. They had no bunker and were living with the farmer in his house. With the arrival of the Cossacks, they had to flee the house. The Jewish couple had a small infant. On their way out of the village in broad daylight the Cossack self-defense force stopped them and all three of them were killed. It was chilling news to us. We had to be more diligent in our daytime guard duty.

The Cossack family headed by young man named Stephan was constantly in and out of the house. As we later found out, Stephan was suspicious from the beginning about the goings-on between the house, the barn and the basement where the pigs were kept. He moved around freely and kept a watchful eye on Jarmolowitz and Magdalena. Once he approached the barn with such speed that Benson had only seconds to get into the Bunker before being discovered. We suspected he might have heard the commotion even though he did not see Benson. On a second occasion we heard him approach the area where the opening to the Bunker was located. We were worried and told the same to our host Jarmolowitz. But we had no choice in the matter. The uninvited Cossacks were here to stay and we had to be on our toes. As the old saying goes "You can hide from a stranger, but from a person living in your own house it is difficult to keep secrets." To our sorrow the saying proved to be true.

On a spring day in 1944, while Benson was in the barn on guard duty, Stephan approached the barn from the rear with such speed that it was humanly impossible for Benson to get into the Bunker in time without being seen. In summer as you come into the barn from the bright sunlight it takes your eyes a couple of seconds to get used to the darkness of the barn. While Stephan could make out the silhouette of a man he didn't have enough time to take a good look at Benson. What he saw was enough for him to discover the entrance to the Bunker. This was the first time that our safety was in real jeopardy.

Stephan did not lose any time telling Jarmolowitz what he had seen, and that a man is hiding in his barn. Jarmolowitz understood what had happened and after the initial shock, composed himself and began to explain the situation to Stephan.

To tell him that he was hiding Jews was unthinkable since the Cossacks were known for their historical hatred of the Jews. While in the village it was common knowledge that Jarmolowitz lost a son to the Nazis, he was now retelling the story to Stephan. He was sure that the Cossack would have more sympathy for his son than for Jews. He told him when the Nazis took his son to be executed, along with 50 other Polish patriots, a miracle happened and his son was only slightly wounded. He was covered with the dead bodies of his colleagues and played dead until the Nazis left. The execution place was in the forest of Scridleve not far from his farm. He managed to return to his father's farm where he had been living in the bunker out of sight of the Nazis.

To Stephan the story was plausible since he was aware of similar stories circulating in other villages. The war news from the front was bad for the Cossacks. Stephan realized the situation presented him with a perfect opportunity to turn against the Nazis. He promised Jarmolowitz to keep his secret in return for a horse and a cow, so when the Germans left he would be able to establish himself on a farm. He hoped that the Red Army and all the Partisans who fought against the Nazis would not overlook the good deed.

After Benson came down into the bunker and told us what happened we all realized we faced a greater emergency than the night my father disappeared. My father's encounter with Novogran happened during the night, so it gave us time in the darkness to leave the bunker if necessary and reach the nearby forest before daybreak. Also the location of the bunker was not compromised. This time we knew that Stephan the Cossack knew the entrance to the bunker.

To leave the bunker in daytime was dangerous since the Cossack self-defense force was stationed in the village. They had guards posted all over the village to stop any infiltration by the Russian Partisans. Every minute now seemed like eternity. We did not know if the Cossack went to see Jarmolowitz or his commanding officer in the village. Your whole life passes before your eyes while waiting, realizing this could be your last day on earth. After so many months and years of suffering, and so close to liberation we were faced with the ultimate challenge. We were waiting for some kind of a sign or signal from Jarmolowitz to help us assess the situation.

One possibility was for us to use the emergency Bunker that we built last summer in preparation for the German army retreat. The emergency bunker was located outside the barn to protect us from being suffocated from smoke inhalation in case the barn was torched. We knew of the German scorched earth policy. Our barn was so close to the main highway. It would be a prime target. By using the emergency bunker we could exit to the open field. This exit from the emergency bunker gave us an extra avenue of escape.

Before long, Jarmolowitz came to see us. He was very agitated and rightfully so since all our lives were at stake. He told us about the conversation he had with Stephan the Cossack. Now our safety was dependent upon another person for whom he could not vouch. Our options were limited, to accept his offer, or prepare to leave the bunker.

We decided to stay and watch for further developments. In one area our position became more tolerable, since Jarmolowitz did not have to hide the food delivery. Stephan even volunteered to bring us some water for washing. On the other hand, Benson was the only one who could reveal himself to the Cossack and the rest of us had to hide. This charade went on for a while until one day Stephan decided that he would like to meet with the younger Jarmolowitz. Benson in his looks and age was similar to the age of Wacek Jarmolowitz. He was the only one left in the bunker while the rest of us moved temporarily to the emergency bunker. He had a cordial meeting with Stephan, after which our food supply has improved. In spring of 1944 the Red Army was getting ready for their summer offensive. We could hear the frequent bombing getting closer to our area. We were anxiously waiting for the day of our liberation.

13

LIBERATION

For about three years we were waiting for the moment of our liberation. We were sure it would happen, but we could not predict the date or time. The entire time period of Nazi occupation lasted only three years, yet looking back now it seemed like a lifetime. It is now more than fifty years since it happened, and the time span has not diminished the imprint on my mind. I still wake up screaming at night reliving some of the frightening experiences I had during the Nazi occupation.

The first inkling we had that our liberation was getting nearer was when we heard the news that the allied invasion of Europe had begun. The German press let their people believe that the so-called Atlantic-Wall *(Fortification the German build on the French coast)* was not penetrable. The first report from the German army was that the allied invasion was stopped dead in its tracks. The farmers listening to the BBC radio knew better. The invasion was massive and successful. Jarmolowitz was very happy with the news and so were we as our ordeal might soon be over. After D-day the Red Army started its summer offensive on the Eastern front.

A couple of weeks later we began to hear the rumbling of the Russian artillery. Being underground in the Bunker the vibration of the ground was even more intensified. Soon after that we began to see the German army in their retreat. The main highway was only couple hundreds yards away from our barn. At the start, the retreat was orderly, later we saw more disoriented groups leaving. The last tank column to pass in front of us had their gun turrets turned to the rear, a sign that they were trying to hold the Russian Army back. The first week of July 1944 the fighting came very close to our village. The explosions of the artillery shells were now more pronounced. The ground began to shake from each explosion. We decided that it was now time to implement our plan to move to the emergency bunker, which was hidden in the open field away from the barn. Should our barn be set on fire then the emergency bunker would provide us with the necessary protection against the smoke and fire. On Saturday July 6, 1944 we began to hear the sound of machine guns and rifle fire. While in the Bunker we could hear the screams of the German soldiers in their hasty retreat. The shooting went on for a whole night and toward morning we could hear Russian being spoken. We were still afraid to leave our Bunker. In the morning a Red Army unit pulled into our back yard. Finally we were free.

Jarmolowitz warned us not to come out yet since the front line was too close to the village and bands of the unorganized German unit were still resisting the Red army. On Sunday morning, we had a conference amongst ourselves and decided that it was time to leave the safety of the bunker and go to our hometown of Nowogrodek. As we were getting ready to leave the Bunker Jarmolowitz asked us not to disclose his name and the place where we were hiding. He feared retribution from the locals, lest they find out that he saved Jews.

This was another terrible awakening that even after we won the war we still lost the battle of hatred and prejudice. The Nazis were defeated but at a terrible cost to us. We were decimated: what was left was only a shadow of the past. Without saying goodbyes to anyone as requested by Jarmolowitz we left the Bunker.

We left the bunker as we came, with the same clothing we wore for the last eighteen months. The shoes were falling apart, so we had to tie them with strings to last us until we got to town. The white color of our shirts turned gray from seldom being washed, and the seams were frayed. The pants were patched over and over again to form a mosaic of patches.

As we were walking toward the city we came across many Red Army soldiers marching to the front lines. Most of them stopped to look at us. We must have been a sight from hell. Our faces were white as snow from not seeing the sun for eighteen months. They assumed that we were prisoners released from some kind of solitary confinement. We told them our story that we were hiding for our lives in an underground bunker for the last year and a half.

As we came into town a crowd of local people surrounded us. They recognized who we were. To them we were ghosts of the past. They assumed that all the Jews in our town were killed and now a few of us showed up to tell our story and it frightened them. Many of them collaborated with the Nazis. Not only did they help them to kill us but also to take over our homes and our possessions. They feared that now they would have to give us back our homes and everything in them. Our homegrown enemies who sought ways to eliminate us surrounded us. A unit of Red Army soldiers from central Asia was passing by us. The unruly mob told them that we were German spies since we spoke Yiddish amongst ourselves, which to them sounded like German. The Red army soldiers were known for their hatred of the Germans and without many questions were ready to execute us. We had to beg them to take us to their commanding officer, hoping that they would be more understanding of our situation. With pointed guns at all of us we were ordered to march to their command post.

Luckily for us the command post had a Red Army doctor who was Jewish. He ordered the soldiers to release us into his custody. Understanding our situation and the danger we faced from the local collaborators, who served as policemen or prison guards, he advised us to find the local militia and stay close to them for protection. We located the building where the militia was stationed. It was across from the market place at the beginning of Grodner Street. Behind was an abandoned house that prior to the war was owned by a Jewish family. The militia turned the house over to us for our use, and it became our permanent residence after liberation.

The front lines were still very close to our city. At night the skies lit up from the bombardment of the Russian artillery and rockets. We were afraid that the Germans may come back, and should this happen; we would retreat with the Russian Army. After a couple of days the sounds from the front lines became more distant and our fears lessened. The Red Army had captured many German Army units. The once arrogant were now meek prisoners of war. A single soldier could control hundreds of them. They were put on display in front of an abandoned store where locals now taunted them and spit in their faces. The once mighty were now helpless. Knowing what the Nazis did to the local people during the occupation the punishment was accepted without protest. The farmers who came to town to see the spectacle made them undress, took the good clothing and shoes and in return gave them some old rags.

I was able to speak to many prisoners and asked why they committed so many atrocities on defenseless civilians. They tried to deny their actions and blamed everything on the Gestapo. I reminded them that it was the German Army who helped the Gestapo in the roundup of the Jews and the Gypsies, that it was German Army trucks that transported my brothers and sisters to their graves. They all suffered from a case of self-induced amnesia. It is amazing what the power of one gun can accomplish. Here were battle-tested German army men being watched over by one young Red army soldier and meekly submitting to his orders.

This may be part of the answer to the question posed to many of the Jewish survivors of why we meekly submitted ourselves to the slaughter by the Nazis. We were not armed nor were we trained militarily to defend ourselves. Psychologically we were lulled into believing that by obeying the German orders we would survive. In our area the Jews finally did organize and they formed the Bielski partisan group, which fought the Nazis in any way possible. By their bold action they were able to save more than a thousand people. We were still only eight surviving Jews in town and were eagerly awaiting the entrance of the Bielski Partisan group. I knew of one uncle and three cousins who were with the Bielski group and wondered how many of them had survived. We heard through the grape vine that the Bielski Partisan group was attacked on the last days before liberation by a German army group and sustained some casualties. Toward the weekend the Bielski Partisan group finally made their entrance into Nowogrodek. It was a sight to remember. The men came on horseback, fully armed while the women and children arrived with the elderly in horse-driven wagons. We were elated to see such a large group of surviving Jews. We kissed and hugged each other. We were glad that we had survived. For the first night the Partisan group settled on the Niankowski farm grounds. The next day we went looking for permanent housing.

There were many dramas being played out that day. Many a young man or woman entered their former homes to find strangers living, where previously their parents lived. Everything in their homes was familiar; the furniture, the utensils and clothing, but no parent remained to help them claim it.

The new residents of the homes were not eager to accommodate. They refused to let the rightful owners reclaim their homes and possessions. Many battles ensued until the authorities had to be called in to settle the disputes. To our sorrow the Communist authorities ruled that unless the new residents were voluntarily willing to abandon our homes, the status quo would prevail. It was ironic that the Communists were now upholding the misdeeds of the Nazi regime, claiming that some of the current residents of our homes were placed there by the order of the Nazis and therefore were personally not involved in confiscating our properties.

The Communist regime adopted the policy where by the Jewish ordeal under the Nazis regime was considered part and parcel of the Nazi misdeeds against the entire Russian population, the victims and the victimizer were put on the same plateau. The atrocities the Nazis committed against the Jewish population with the help of many local collaborators were looked upon only in the context of atrocities against Soviet citizens.

This was the first indication we had that Stalin's policy toward the Jews was not far removed from the policies of the Nazi party. The denial of the Holocaust against the Jewish population is a dark chapter of Stalinist anti-Semitism. Nazi collaborators could only be prosecuted if their misdeeds were against Soviet citizens. The mass graves scattered all over the pale of Byelorussia, Ukraine and Russia, where 100% of the victims were Jews did not matter. The markers on the graves were those of Soviet citizens thereby overlooking the unique Jewish suffering. To the embarrassment of many Soviet intellectuals the Communist were playing to the nationalist mood of the Russian people.

After the first week of our liberation the reality of our great loss became more evident. Every house and every street corner reminded us of someone who was not here anymore. My childhood friends, my school friends, they are all gone never to be seen again. The most difficult part was to come to terms with my mother's and my younger brother Osher's demise. Somewhere in my subconscious I did not want to accept the fact that they were killed. I fantasized that my mother escaped the slaughter and was hiding somewhere, soon to reveal herself.

Soon the reality of our loss gave way to depression, but not for long. A new challenge was handed to us. The war with Nazi Germany was still raging, with great losses on both sides of the fighting. The Russian army needed replacements. In Nowogrodek, as in all other liberated towns, an official proclamation was placed all over town instructing all men ages eighteen to fifty to report to the draft board. Myself my brother and my father were all eligible for the draft. After all our suffering during the Nazi occupation, our lives could be placed back in jeopardy. We knew of the tremendous number of losses the Red Army was sustaining in fighting the Germans. But how can you refuse a chance to fight the Nazis?

My father, because of his age was given a job with the local fire department exempting him from the draft. My brother and myself joined the thousands of other men reporting to the draft.

14

LIFE IN THE RED ARMY

A new chapter of our suffering was unfolding. After registering with the local board we were ordered to report for induction. We were given instruction to leave the city of Nowogrodek and to report to the nearest railroad link, which was located at the time in the city of Stolpce. As no transportation was provided for the draftees, we had to march about fifty miles on foot to reach our first destination. We left Nowogrodek on a Wednesday afternoon and after marching a number of miles toward our destination we settled down for our first night of rest in an open field. Open fires sprung up all around us as the men prepared their evening meal.

The food we brought along was meager, and the farm people helped us with their more bountiful provisions. Our bodies were so depleted from years of starvation during the German occupation that our feet soon gave up on the idea of marching all the way to Stolpce. Luckily so many empty army trucks were returning from delivering provisions to the front lines, that we were able to thumb our way to Stolpce. We arrived days ahead of the other draftees in our group, giving us a chance to rest for a few days.

In Stolpce we had to register again because the registration papers from

1945: Paul, Russian Army, East Germany.

Nowogrodek were not forwarded. It was the first indication of the disorganization of the Red Army.

While we lingered in Stolpce for almost a week, our food reserves were running low because no food was provided for us by the military. The news of our food crisis must have filtered home to our father. He arranged with our cousin Paula to deliver more food to us. As fate should have it, this was the last time I would see Paula after our liberation in 1944, until we met again in 1972 in Israel. After registering all over again we boarded a troop transport train on the first leg of our journey to the hinterland of mother Russia and father Stalin.

The train ride into the hinterland of Russia lasted for days. The first major stop was the city of Minsk. The destruction of war was visible all over. The railroad station was bombed out and destroyed. The fences around the station and the nearby houses were all gone. We looked for pieces of wood so that we could start a fire and cook our food, but we could not find any. The travelers before us must have used up every piece of wood in the vicinity of the railroad station. We could not venture too far for fear that the train would leave without us.

The next big stop was the city Of Smolensk. As we were approaching the city you could see all the trenches the German and the Russian Armies left behind. The city of Smolensk changed hands many times during the German onslaught on Russia, and the scars of war were visible all over. Some of the trenches were left intact for future generations to see.

Our final destination was the city of Bryansk. The area between Bryansk and Orel was the places where the fierce tank battles took place during the war. We could still see the burned out hulls of hundreds of Russian and German tanks scattered all over the landscape.

The city of Bryansk was a drab colorless industrial town. The military camp was on the outskirts of the city. The camp was enclosed with a barbed wire fence. The entrance by the main gate had a guardhouse. Every one entering and leaving the military camp was searched and checked. The housing for the military was in old pre-revolutionary buildings. They had no running water or toilet facilities. The outhouses were nearby in an open field. The river in the middle of the city served as the washing facility. Each morning after get up time we were given two minutes to dress only to the waist and then run to the river to wash ourselves. In the cold winter month we had to break the ice to get to the water underneath.

After washing ourselves we returned to the camp, finished dressing and assembled in the dining area for breakfast. Each company delegated two or three soldiers to go the kitchen for our food. In the morning the food consisted of hot tea, a chunk of bread and a spoonful of sugar. We had no utensils; the hot tea came in rusted pail which was shared by all. The sugar was handed each one of us in the palm of our hand, some-times before or after having our tea. We licked our hands clean to the last kernel. The bread was dark and soggy because the civilian kitchen crew used to steal some of the flour and mix in potatoes instead.

After breakfast the new recruits were marched out to the open fields for basic training. The training field was about five kilometers from the barracks. Besides military training which was vigorous and physically exhausting, we were also given political indoctrination. The classroom was the open field. The recruits sat in a semi-circle in a knee-high trench, with the bare ground serving as make-believe chairs. The instructor standing in the middle could watch over all of us. This noontime lecture gave everyone a chance to rest before we headed back to the military compound.

Looking around in the open field we were able to meet our comrades in-arms. To our astonishment we came across some hometown friends who during the German occupation collaborated with the Nazis. Their presence in the army disturbed us. My brother and I discussed this amongst us and decided to take action. We contacted the commanding officer and told him about our fears of the collaborators. He put us in touch with the internal security officer who took down our testimony as to the activities of the known Nazi collaborators.

Among the collaborators were two sets of brothers. One set of brothers served as Prison guards in the city of Nowogrodek while the other set of brothers served as policemen under the local SS during the German occupation. Surprisingly the security officer already had some testimony from other soldiers and a long file on the activities of the Nazi collaborators.

For a time nothing was said to us about the collaborators, and we continued with our military training. About a month later my brother and myself were ordered to report to Headquarters. As we traveled to the Headquarters of our Red Army unit we noticed that some of the collaborators were also traveling with us.

When all of us reported to the Army Headquarters, we were asked to appear before an Army tribunal. One by one we were called into a hearing room. We faced a tribunal of high Brass. We were asked to repeat our testimony as to the activities of the Nazi collaborators during the German occupation. Standing in one corner was the accused; all their military insignias were removed from their uniforms including their belts and shoelaces.

They were asked if they hold or held personal animosity toward us. The answer was no. After our testimony and the testimony from other soldiers the accused admitted their guilt, but qualified that they were forced by the Germans to commit the atrocities against the Partisans and other citizens. After a short deliberation by the Top Brass the verdict was guilty as charged. Two of the collaborators who personally executed Russian Partisan were given the death penalty. The rest received prison terms of hard labor up to twenty years. This was the last time we saw the collaborators. All the witnesses were given orders to return to their military units. Our training continued until the end of 1944.

In January of 1945 we were given travel orders to report to the front lines. We were about to begin the final battle to destroy the Nazi beast on its own territory. The entire Eighth army of fighting men with all their supporting supplies and equipment were loaded onto freight cars for the journey to the front line. About forty soldiers were loaded into one freight car. The Army supplied us with wooden boards to construct bunks in the cars so that we could have a place to sleep. Each freight car was given a wood-burning stove to keep us warm.

January is pretty cold in Russia and it took us a while to get the inside of the car warmed up. The frozen wooden bunks began to thaw, and the melting of the ice on the boards turned into water. This was a great discomfort for the soldiers, and many of us caught colds.

After leaving Bryansk the train headed towards Gomel, then towards the former Soviet-Polish border until the outskirts of Warsaw. Before Warsaw we had to disembark the train because the wooden bridge traversing the river Vistula was not strong enough to allow the locomotive to cross the bridge. The empty cars were pushed across the bridge by the locomotive and another one picked up the car on the other side of the river. Once the cars were over the river the soldiers were allowed to traverse the bridge on foot.

After crossing the bridge we again boarded the freight cars on our journey to Germany. The last big stop was Poznian, and from there it was only hours from the former Polish and German border. We disembarked across the German border in the city of Starnberg. This was as far as the train would travel.

We arrived in late afternoon. The town appeared empty of people. We were billeted in abandoned private homes. As the evening set in we realized

that the electric power was off. We had to find our way in the dark. The first
night we slept on an empty floor. The next morning after breakfast we were
ordered to the bathhouse to take our first shower in days. The showers were
set up in the bathroom of a big private house. To keep the house warm the
soldiers started a fire in the fireplace. The smoke from the chimney caught the
attention of a German spotter plane. They directed some mortar shells on to
the house. This was the end of the shower house, the army changed back to
using the outdoor open air showers.

The food at the field kitchen was a big improvement from the food we
received in Russia. The German Army left storehouses full of food from all
over Europe. The Red Army soldiers helped themselves to whatever they
could find. It came to the point that some of the soldiers stopped coming to
the field kitchen. The warehouse was full of cigarettes, liquor and French
wines.

For a short while we had a ball. After a couple days of rest we were
marched from Starnberg toward our final destination, which at the time was
the front line, bordering the city of Frankfurt on the river Oder.

As we marched towards Frankfurt we came to a fork in the road. The highway separated in two different directions. My brothers unit went in a north-
westerly direction while my unit was marching to the southwest. Without
realizing it my brother and myself were separated. The army for obvious reason to avoid two brothers from being hurt at the same time ordered the sepa-
ration of brothers.

Our road took us directly to the outskirts of the city of Frankfurt on the
Oder River. From our positions we could observe the city but we refrained
from attacking it, because the German planes dropped leaflets informing us
that the city has stores of poison gas, which accidentally could be released. We
were in a defensive position in some concrete slab bunkers and connecting
trenches.

The Russian army had learned from its past mistakes and now formed a triple line of defensive positions. Should the first line be broken through by the
German army there would be a second and third line of defense. The new
recruits were given a taste of the war by first being placed in the third defensive line, later in the second line and finally in the front line.

As my unit was being advanced from one position to the next, I bumped in
to my cousin Daniel whose unit was stationed in a nearby concrete bunker.
There was occasional shooting and aerial bombardments and probing by our
and the enemy's scout units. We were advised to be especially alert at night. It

was then that the scouts were more active trying to secure a *"thong"*. In army lingo this meant to capture a live soldier for interrogation about upcoming plans.

One night I was shot at because my bayonet was shining in the moonlight and the Germans noticed it. After this experience I kept my rifle at a lower position to avoid being seen. The food from the field kitchen was delivered twice a day, at dawn and at dusk. In the gray of the morning or evening it was safe to approach our trenches provided you knew the password, otherwise we had order to shoot on sight. The password was changed daily to avoid a breach of security.

Because of the abundance of the supplies in Germany the army was well fed to the point where some of us got sick with diarrhea. After informing my commanding officer of my problem I was ordered to report to the field hospital for observation. The standard treatment in the army was to put you on strict diet of dried bread and tea. In most cases this was enough to cure the disease.

Before being discharged from the field hospital the nurse took my temperature as a routine precaution. The nurse informed me that I was running a fever and therefore could not be discharged. After a few more days of rising temperature two doctors examined me. They confirmed that I was sick and needed further treatment. The doctor's decision was to evacuate me to the rear of the front to an army hospital, which was better equipped to treat my illness. The ambulance, which was taking me to the hospital, was full with severely wounded soldiers. Their moans and groans I still remember. I felt out of place with my body intact and no signs of injury but running a high fever.

Upon arriving at the hospital the doctors of the triage separated the patients according to the severity of their wounds. I landed in a room full of sick soldiers all suffering from internal sicknesses. The doctor on duty examined me. After the examination the doctor informed me that I was still running a high fever and that I was suffering from a severe cold with the possibility that my lungs might be involved.

Since this hospital didn't have any X-ray machines I was transported to a military hospital in the city of Lodz in Poland, which had the necessary equipment.

By the time I got to Lodz I was pretty sick and needed immediate attention. Two male doctors examined me but could not decide on the diagnosis. They called upon the expertise of an older woman doctor. The woman doctor, after examining me with a wooden tube-like listening device against my chest, informed me that I was suffering from pleurisy. The illness would require a prolonged stay in the hospital. All my suffering from the forced labor camps under the Nazis and the confinement in a bunker for eighteen months were finally catching up with my health and me. After a few weeks of rest and better food and with aspirin-like medicine I began to feel better.

The war with Germany ended while I was still in the hospital in Lodz. I remember the day and the first night as the soldiers of Poland and Russia celebrated the end of the war. The soldiers fired their rifles in the air to celebrate the victory over Nazism. Some of the bullets hit the overhead electrical wires and our hospital was left in the dark until morning.

Now my concern turned to my brother and my father whose whereabouts I did not know. The war has ended, and I am alive. But is my brother still alive? His unit and mine were engaged in the battle of Berlin.

Unknown to me at that time, my father being a Polish citizen was evacuated from Nowogrodek to Lodz, and was living only a few miles from the military hospital.

I was constantly mailing letters to my father in Russia informing him that I am alive and did he have any mail from my brother, who was still in the Russian army.

15

RUSSIAN ZONE East Germany—Back Home
NOWOGRODEK

The Second World War ended while I was still hospitalized at a military hospital in Lodz. The end of the war gave a psychological lift to all of us. One patient on the ward managed to get a bottle of vodka, and we all shared in the celebration with a toast. The nurse assigned to the ward happened to come in while the celebration was going on. One of the patients made an uncomplimentary comment to the nurse. The consequence of this was that the nurse reported the drinking incident to the supervising doctor. The doctor instituted an inquiry, questioning each patient separately. Also all of the involved patients were given a thorough medical examination to evaluate their medical condition. The result was that many of us, including myself, were informed that because of our drinking of vodka and not following medical orders, we were being discharged from the hospital.

I was still not fully recovered but had no choice but to leave the hospital. I was handed an envelope with my medical records and was asked if I wanted to go to my hometown or return to the unit I served in East Germany. I chose to go to Germany hoping to find my brother or my cousin who I believed were some place in East Germany. My first stop was Berlin. The city was in ruins; the streets were full with rubble of the collapsed buildings. All over were signs of the war and its aftermath.

In Fuerstenwalde near Berlin I was given travel orders by Army Headquarters to proceed to Dresden to catch up with my unit. In Dresden I saw the results of the most destructive allied bombing of the war. On both sides of the river Elbe, which divided the city all you could see were the skeletons of bombed and burned out buildings. Young children roamed the city begging for food. I found my unit stationed in what was once the home of the Dresdener Bank. To make place in the building for army offices, we were ordered to take out boxes full with German banknotes and burn them in a bonfire. Months later I found out that the paper money we burned were still legal tender in Germany.

From Dresden we were given orders to march to Chemnitz and on to Weimar. It took us weeks of marching on foot to reach our destination. In Chemnitz I overheard a German woman remark, when she saw the ragtag Russian army enter the city," that it is unbelievable that this primitive looking army could defeat the well-organized German army".

From Chemnitz we marched to Weimar. I still remember that some of the main roads had fruit trees planted on both sides of the highway and to my amazement the locals didn't disturb the fruit on the trees. The Russian soldiers took the liberty to pick the fruit off the trees and in the process wasted more than they could eat.

Weimar and the nearby university town of Jena were spared the massive war destruction of other German cities. In Weimar I ventured out on the town and strolled in the shade of the trees, which lined the boulevards. I met with some locals, and in my discussions with them I questioned them about the Nazi atrocities and how much they knew about it. Each and every one denied any knowledge and blamed it all on the leader of the Nazi party. With Buchenwald being so close to the general area I doubted their truthfulness.

The first time I saw American soldiers was when my Army unit entered the city of Jena. The American army liberated the city of Jena. With the end of the war it was transferred to the Russian Zone. According to the allied agreement Germany was divided into four occupation Zones. The Eastern part of Germany was the Russian zone, and the western part of Germany was divided among the American, British and French zones.

In Jena I saw a column of American trucks loaded with supplies leaving the city. Many of the truck drivers were African American which was a novelty for me since I never before, except for the movies, seen a black person.

Life in Weimar and Jena was functioning as if there was never a war. The leadership of the cities was now in the hands of the German communists, supervised by Red army personnel. Before the Americans left the Russian zone they released all the German POW's. It was now the task of the Red Army to go into the field to round up the former German soldiers and other Germans suspected in Nazi atrocities. Because of my knowledge of German and Russian I was given the task of translator.

The Red army staged their sweeps in the early morning hours. After entering the village, a group of Red Army soldiers would pay a visit to the so-called *"Burgermeister"* the Mayor of the village informing him of our task and asking for assistance. In most cases the Mayors or head of the villages complied, supplying us with necessary information on former German POW's and Nazi collaborators.

One incident I still remember vividly. In one of the villages we received information that a former POW is hiding out on a farm. It was early in the morning when we went to the farm. The farmhouse was of a typical German style, painted white with a brown wooden rectangular frame. A white picket fence all around the house and brown shutters on the windows. We quietly unlocked the gate and came to a locked front door.

We knocked on the door and asked whoever was inside to open. We must have caught the farm people by surprise because after a few minutes we heard a female voice asking us to wait until she was dressed. In meantime the soldiers made an inspection around the house, everything looked peaceful and quiet.

When the door to the house opened we saw a young woman accompanied by an older man. They identified themselves as a father and daughter. We asked for permission to enter the house and told the lady of our task to inspect the house for any former POW's. While in the house the lady offered to prepare breakfast for all of us, which we graciously accepted. After breakfast we asked the young lady again if anyone else was living in the house. She answered us that she and her father were the sole occupants of the farm.

Before leaving the house the Sergeant in charge of our company suggested that we check the upstairs of the house. The Sergeant and myself walked up the stairs where to the right of the landing, we saw two doors that seemed to us to be two separate bedrooms. We opened one door and looked inside. The room was dark since the shutters were still closed. It took us a moment for our eyes to get adjusted to the dim light in the room. In the corner we saw a made up bed. It looked like the room was empty. We took a few more steps inside and looked again to the right and the left, satisfying ourselves that no one was there.

As we turned around to leave the room a man standing behind the opened door surprised us. We pointed our guns toward him and ordered him to step out from behind the door. One of the men's hands was in a white cast and a sling made out from gauze, around his neck. Otherwise he was in good shape, slim and trim, and he looked to be in the early thirties. We checked him for arms and, finding none, ordered him to step down to the kitchen.

In the kitchen we confronted the young lady and her father with our find. They denied knowing that the man was there. They claimed that he must have entered the house without their knowledge. The excuse did not sit right with my Sergeant who immediately ordered the old man out of the house. He told me to inform the young lady that her father will be shot for hiding escaped Nazis.

I ordered the man out in the yard and walked him down to the fence. Two army buddies were ready to carry out the Sergeant's order. While I was marching the old man to his execution the young lady ran out of the house, caught up with me and fell at my feet, begging me to spare her father's life since it was she that let her relative into the house without her father's knowledge. Her unrelenting crying and begging made me stop. For a moment it reminded me of my mother begging a German soldier when they entered our town not to harm her children. Now I was the soldier and another woman was begging me to spare her father's life. I asked my soldier friends to stop, and let us talk again to our Sergeant. I related to him her story but he was adamant in his order to execute the old man. I finally put up my own argument saying that I understand how he feels, since he and myself lost relatives to the Nazi atrocities. This time we had the upper hand, and we should not act like Nazis.

My Sergeant was outraged. Since I was Jewish he felt I should support his decision. The war had ended and I could not see myself killing another person. I offered to take both of the prisoners to the commanding officer and let him make the final decision. After a long argument of pro and con, the Sergeant relented and let us march the prisoners to the army command post. At the command post we found many former POW's assembled. After hearing our story the wounded man was taken to the stockade with the rest of the German POW's. The old man was released with a warning not to hide any more POW's; the threat of execution was enough of a punishment for his misdeeds. To this day I know that I saved the man's life.

After this incident we were ordered to return back to our military base. In future raids to search for hidden Nazis and former POW's, some guilty Germans attempted to escape punishment by hiding in the nearest forest. They thus took a page out of tactics of the Russian partisans to avoid capture. The Russian military became aware of the scheme and we were ordered to comb the nearby forest. We did capture some Germans and because of their action they were arrested and many were exiled to Siberia.

I remember entering a village and came across a house where we once captured a German POW. We entered the house for a short rest. The lady of the house was very friendly. She offered to prepare breakfast, and we cordially accepted. After finishing the breakfast we thanked her for her hospitality and were ready to leave.

Since I was the only one who spoke German she asked me what happened to her husband who was taken away in one of the prior raids. I could have lied to her and told her that he will return in a couple of weeks, but this would have been the same tactics the former Nazis used on us. I decided to level with her and told her that most of the able-bodied men were taken back to Russia to help rebuild the destroyed cities like Stalingrad and that it will take between five to ten years to accomplish the task. The lady fainted in front of me, and we had to revive her. I question myself if false hope would have been better than the truth.

Once I got settled in Weimar I received news that my cousin Daniel was stationed in Jena. One Sunday morning I took a short trip to visit him. He was glad to see me, and we had a chance to catch up with all that had happened to us the last couple of months. What he did not tell me and what I found out 27 years later when I saw him in Tel Aviv-Israel was, that he planned to escape from the Russian army soon after my visit.

A couple of weeks after I saw my cousin Daniel I was called to be interrogated by an officer of the Russian army intelligence unit. They questioned me about the whereabouts of my cousin. I was puzzled by their concern and told them that to the best of my knowledge he is still stationed in Jena. I gave them the number of his regiment and unit and told them of my Sunday visit with him, which I am sure they knew about. All the questioning by the officer did not make sense to me at the time, but became clear to me 27 years later.

I was still looking for my brother, but had no luck finding his unit of the Russian army. One morning while I was reading the Russian newspaper *"Pravda"* I came across an article in the form of a proclamation by the Russian and English governments. Both countries agreed to help repatriate all former Polish citizens who lived in the territories of prewar Poland, from western Russia back to Poland. The war was over, and I had no intention of staying in Russia. Without realizing the risk involved in wanting to leave the workers paradise I formally applied to be evacuated back to the new Poland.

My commanding officer was puzzled by my application and he called me in for a face-to-face interview. He quietly let on to me that what I was doing was very risky. Since I was Jewish and not Polish I could wind up in Siberia. I explained to him that my religion should not pose a problem since the article quoted from the newspaper Pravda talked only about citizenship and not religion. I was a native-born Polish citizen and therefore had the right, according to the article, to request a transfer from Russia back to Poland. He asked to see the article I was referring to, and after reading it to himself he promised to forward my application to army Headquarters. In meantime he ordered me to return to my unit to wait for further instructions.

About three weeks later I was called back to his office and given two hours to collect my belongings and be ready to be shipped out to the Polish Army. To some extent I felt relieved. The Polish army was better then Siberia. From Weimar an army truck took me to Buchenwald, the former Nazi death camp. Above the entrance to the camp was the wrought iron sign, which read *"Arbeit macht frei"* work would set you free.

The Russian army was using the outer camp as an assembly point for different nationals who served in the Russian Army. I came across nationals from more then a dozen countries, all of them waiting to be discharged or transferred to their respective countries of origin.

I was sitting in the registration room waiting to register, when an officer came out and asked the assembled for volunteers to help with the office work. One of the requirements was the proper knowledge of the Russian language, because we will be processing many documents pertaining to the transfer or discharge of soldiers.

I raised my hand to volunteer, and was assigned to the office of the commanding Russian General. I was handed stacks of Red Army identification cards. Each stock of card had to be sorted according to nationality or country of origin. Many older Russian nationals who served in the Red Army for more than four years were also being demobilized and discharged from the Red Army. In each case I had to figure out the duration of travel time for each soldier to return to his hometown. Some soldiers were going as far as the Far East and were given provisions and coupons to last them all the way home.

In the process of sorting all the documents I came across my own identification papers. It was among the army books destined to be stamped with the transfer stamp, to be transferred to the Polish army. It was a momentary decision by me, and, instead of stamping the document with the transfer stamp, I used the demobilized stamp. I handed all the documents to the General for him to sign. He signed them all including mine. I was free to go home.

I spent one more day visiting the village of Buchenwald. I spoke to the locals and asked them if they knew of the atrocities going on in the concentration camp during the war. All of them denied any knowledge. They acknowl-edged that foreign labor was being used in the camp to work in the underground munitions factories, and this was all they knew. I did not believe them then, nor do I believe them now. The proximity of the camp to the vil-lage was so close that they could see. Surely they could smell the stench com-ing from the death camp.

Next morning I went to the army PX and received my provisions according to my order of travel and was on my way back home to Nowogrodek. I took the train from Berlin to Warsaw and from Warsaw to Baranovich and from Baranovich to Novojelna. In Novojelna I had to change trains from the Big train to the Small train for the final leg of my journey to Nowogrodek. The German army built the train from Novojelna to Nowogrodek during the First World War, when the front lines were not far from the city. The small rail-road line continued to Lubcz a small town on the river Niemen. Here during the First World War the German army held a defensive position for more than three years and used the new railroad to transport supplies to their troops at the front.

The train was very familiar to me because during my youth I took many vacation trips to the pine forest of Novojelna where the TOZ, a Jewish health organization, run a summer camp for school age children. The railroad cars were filled with passengers. The farmers now used the train to transport their goods to Nowogrodek, including eggs, butter and some live chickens.

In the four years of the war the dynamics of the area changed. The Jews, who represented about fifty per cent of the prewar traveling public, were gone. I felt lonely and sad. With trepidation in my heart, I finally reached Nowo-grodek.

I went to the house where my father lived when I left town only to find out that he was long gone to Lodz, Poland. A distant cousin of mine who was traveling back and forth from Russia To Poland advised me of my father's whereabouts in Lodz and was willing to guide me to him.

First I had to register with the authorities of the city to receive my ration coupons. As a result of the war food and clothing and any bare necessities of life were still being rationed. My father's friends, who now lived in the house, shared their meager rations with me. I felt obligated to repay them. They advised me that the local post office was holding some packages for my father, which arrived after my father left Russia. The packages were the ones I mailed him from Germany and now would be very useful to me. I went to the local post office, identified myself and asked for the packages. The Postmaster hesitated to release them since they were addressed to my father and not to me, but since I was the sender I claimed them to be mine. After a short deliberation I realized that the Postmaster wanted a share of my goods. I agreed to open the packages in his presence and allowed him to take some shirts and underwear. I sold the rest of the goods on the open market. The money helped me to sustain myself while I was in Russia and on the trip back to Poland.

First I had to receive permission to leave Russia. My friend advised me that an evacuation train was leaving Russia for Poland in about three days. I put some pressure on the local official to grant me permission to leave. I was now a war veteran and claimed some of my privileges. Permission was granted and after three days I was ready to leave.

The last three days I spent in my hometown were very depressing. Besides not finding my father I was again faced with the great loss we sustained in the war. There was not a street or house I passed by that did not remind my of a friend or relative who was killed by the Nazis during the war. We won the war but lost the battle. The many happy years of my youth were now overshadowed with pain and sorrow; I stood in the market place overlooking a cemetery. It was more than a human being can endure, and after three days I was more than ready to leave town.

I joined a group of evacuees going to Novojelna where an evacuation train was being assembled for the trip to Poland. The majority of evacuees were Polish farmers. The farmers loaded up the train with all their earthly possessions including their livestock. Two friends and myself I met at the train traveled light. All our possessions were in our suitcases. The evacuation train stopped at every station to feed and water the livestock, making the journey which ordinarily should take one day drag on for a couple of weeks.

Once we reached Warsaw we left the evacuation train and took a connecting passenger train to Lodz. In Lodz one of my traveling companions took me to my father's apartment. My father was surprised and overjoyed to see me. I took a bath, which I sorely needed and went straight to bed. It was more than four years when I last slept in a comfortable bed with a quilt cover. I thought that I would sleep for weeks to make up for all the sleepless nights of the war, but to my surprise I was up the very next morning. My father had breakfast ready for me, and after breakfast I took a stroll down to the center of town on Pietrokowska Avenue. I was amazed with the normalcy of life in the city. After all the suffering I endured during the war, the Nazi occupation, the mass murders, the year and a half in the bunker and the more than a year in the army, I now faced the adjustment back to civilian life.

Earning a living was far from my mind, but my father soon introduced me to reality. He handed me a suitcase with saccharin to take to a local dealer. It was the first of many business deals in postwar Poland. My father and myself soon came to the conclusion that Poland was not the place for us to start anew. As soon as my brother Paul would leave the Polish army and join us we would leave Poland.

16

GEORGE and PAUL—POLAND 1945

It was about November 1945 when I received a letter from my brother Paul that he was transferred from the Russian army to the Polish army. His army unit was stationed in the port city of Stettin on the Baltic Sea. This former German city was now under Polish control. The German population in the city was being prodded by the Polish authorities to leave town. Accepting the reality that the city is now part of the new Poland many German nationals left. Stettin was part and parcel of the former Third Reich now being dismantled, according to the agreement among the victorious Allies. Poland was being compensated for territories ceded to the Soviet Union in the East. The western borders of the new Poland were moved to the so named "Oder-Niese" line. The rivers formed a natural demarcation line separating the new Poland from Germany.

In Stettin, some German nationals refused to accept reality and continued to resist the Polish authorities. I was warned before I left Lodz for Stettin about snipers still operating in the vicinity of the city. Regardless of the lurking dangers I decided to go to see my brother Paul.

Amongst the Jewish survivors in Poland I came across a friend whose brother was also stationed with the Polish Army in Stettin. The two of us agreed to travel together. To make our travel easier, we donned our Old Russian army uniforms. Dressed in Russian uniforms you could travel free on all the railroads in Poland.

We left Lodz on a Sunday Morning on a train going to Warsaw. In Warsaw we changed trains. We took the train to Poznian and from Poznian to Stettin. We arrived in Stettin in the early evening.

The city was still under curfew. We had to find a place to stay overnight. We left the train station on foot and not far from the station we came across an apartment building. The building seemed to be in fairly good condition. The front door to the entrance of the building was open. My traveling companion and myself decided to check out the place for overnight accommodation. We entered the building and saw a flight of steps leading to the first floor. The two of us walked up the stairs and entered the hallway. On the right side was a door, which seemed to be an entrance to an apartment. I knocked on the door to the right of the hallway. For a while there was no answer. We knocked again and waited. We soon heard the clicking of the door lock and the dangling of a chain.

Slowly the door opened. Through the narrow opening we could see the face of an older woman. The woman spoke German. We introduced ourselves and asked if we may stay in her place overnight, and offered to pay for the lodging. She agreed to let us stay overnight in her apartment, but she warned us that the bedroom is very cold since no heat was provided for the apartment. Our choices were limited and we agreed to stay in the cold bedroom. She offered us more quilts to keep us warm for the night. We took off our coats and shoes and lay down in bed with our clothing on. We covered ourselves with the quilts, and, being tired from the daylong train ride, we soon fell asleep.

In the morning we woke up to the smell of fresh coffee. We got dressed and came into the kitchen. The lady of the house had hot coffee and breakfast ready for us. In the morning while in our bedroom we noticed many, what looked like family pictures on the walls. Many of the men in the pictures were dressed in German military uniforms. We asked the lady of the house; who were the people in the pictures. She willingly took us around the room and pointed out her sons who were in the German army. One of them she said was killed on the Russian front, and another one was killed on the western front. We offered her our condolences and told her what a shame that so many young men had to die because of a misguided policy of the German government. We told her about our suffering and the loss of life during the Nazi occupation. While we felt sorry for her, we pointed out that the Germans started the war, and now the innocent have to pay for it.

I had my brother's address in Stettin and asked the lady of the house for direction to my destination. She gave me a number of a trolley car which stopped not far from the apartment and advised me to take the car all the way to end of the line and look for the address. We thanked the lady for her hospitality and left.

The trolley station was not far from the building where we had stayed for the night. As we approached the station we saw the car with the proper number coming to a stop. Without asking for more directions we jumped on to the trolley car and were on our way to find my brother.

The trip was long and we enjoyed the scenery. When we arrived at the final stop we could see a wide stretch of seawater. I asked the conductor for direction to my brother's address. He explained to me that while we took the right numbered line this trolley car went in the opposite direction, therefore we would have to take the same trolley car back all the way in the reverse direction. We finally arrived at the section of the city where the Polish army was stationed.

I knew that my brother Paul was transferred to the communication section of the Polish army. His knowledge of Polish and Russian came in handy in his position, since the army itself was Polish but the upper level of command was Russian.

On the way to the military compound I met two Polish soldiers and asked them to help me find the place where my brother was stationed. They pointed to an area, which looked more residential than military. The communication section of the Polish army was located in what were formerly residences of German officials.

As I came close to the area I found a military guard blocking the street. I explained to him my mission and gave him the name of my brother, requesting his help. He pointed out to me one of the houses where my brother's unit was quartered. It was a one-story brick house with a walk down basement. The door to the downstairs was open, I saw a military man standing in the doorway looking at me. For a moment we did not recognize each other.

My brother ran up the stairs to greet me. I last saw my brother more than ten months ago in the city of Starenberg. Then he wore a Russian uniform, now he was wearing a Polish uniform with the insignia of the communication core. We were very happy to see each other and spent some time reminiscing and exchanging stories of the last ten months. I told my brother that my mission was to take him home to see our father.

We knew of a standing order, which allowed any draftee, who had not seen his parents for more than a year, to receive two weeks furlough to visit his family. To obtain his leave, my brother first had to receive permission from his commanding officer. The commanding officer wasn't eager to see my brother go. It was close to the Christmas Holiday and many soldiers were asking for furlough. My brother had yardage of fine English wool for a suit. He offered it as a gift to his commanding officer. The bribe helped. His superior agreed to give him two weeks leave to visit his family, with a promise from my brother that he would return on time.

Once my brother received his permission to leave we did not waste any time and on the same day took the train back to Lodz. My father was over-joyed to see the two of us back in Lodz.

After a good night rest my brother went out on the town. He was amazed to see civilian life functioning again in the city especially on Pietrokowska Avenue where all the shops and bakeries were located. While walking down the avenue he came across a Polish officer. He passed the officer without saluting him. The officer called my brother back and ordered him to march three times back and forth, and salute him. After this episode my brother decided to discard his military uniform and go back to civilian clothing.

17

LEAVING POLAND for the AMERICAN ZONE WEST GERMANY

Our time was running short; we had less than two weeks left for my brother to return to his army unit. We notified the Jewish underground operation "BRICHA" that we were ready to leave Poland. Everything was now happening quickly. We were advised to be ready to leave Poland on a moment's notice. My father made arrangements to sell his apartment. We packed our personal belongings to the extent that we could carry them ourselves. Everything else had to be left over or sold. The orders from the Bricha came sooner than expected, forcing us to leave without ever receiving the money for my father's apartment.

Our travel orders were to take the train from Lodz to Waldenburg on a scheduled time. On the station in Lodz we were to look for a tall man in a black hat with a group of about 50 people traveling together. When the train from Warsaw stopped in Lodz there were hundreds of people on and off the train. Nowhere could we find our leader and his group of travelers. The train leaving for Waldenburg was overflowing with people; it seemed that the whole country was traveling. There was no way we could board the train in a normal manner since the entrance to the passenger cars were blocked. We pushed our father through an open window into a car, and my brother and myself traveled in style on the roof of the train. We laid low on the roof of the car with our backpacks in front of us as a protecting shield from the cold wind. We arrived in Waldenburg chilled to the bone.

Again we looked for our man with his group of refugees. To our dismay he was nowhere to be found. Hundreds of passengers disembarked from the train and soon left the train station. As the platform of the train station began to empty we noticed the Polish Police patrolling the station. We had been fore-warned not to loiter too long on the train platform due to local Police vigi-lance, which specifically looked for A.W.O.L. soldiers. My brother was now one of them. We left the station not knowing where we were heading.

On our way out of the station, we came across a Jewish couple that were visiting a relative in Waldenburg. We told them about our predicament, they offered to take us to their brother's house to stay overnight. The brother's wife had given birth to twins and they had come to see them. It was a joy for us to see the twins and to acknowledge life after so much death and destruction.

After the end of the war, many Jewish survivors of the holocaust traveled from city to city in search of relatives. Amongst the Jewish survivors a code word was adopted. The word was *"Amcho"* which in Hebrew means "your peo-ple". By using the code word you could find out who amongst the crowds of people was Jewish.

We spent the night with our newfound Jewish friends. On the morning after breakfast we were out on the town in Waldenburg looking for our leader and his group of refugees. The family we stayed with told us, that a Jewish organization in Waldenburg offered help to Jews wanting to settle in the city and build a new life in Poland. We were also warned not to divulge our plans to them, but we hoped to find out about the refugee group who arrived in town last night.

We took the trolley car to the address of the Jewish organization, arriving to our destination about noontime. We found a Jewish straggler hanging around the building of the organization that heard about the "Bricha" group operating in Waldenburg, but they could not or would not tell us the exact location from which they operated.

We left the building of the local Jewish organization and took the trolley back to the center of the city. When we arrived at the stop in the center of town my brother Paul and I managed to get off the trolley car. The incoming crowd pushed my father back, compelling him to stay in the car. For the moment we were concerned about him, but we assumed that he would have enough understanding to get off the car at the next stop and return to us. In meantime we stood close to the trolley car stop awaiting his return.

While standing there a man approached us and asked us if by any chance our name is Lubow. When we answered affirmatively he was overjoyed. He told me he had scouts looking for us all over town. As soon as our father returned and came off the trolley car we told him the good news that we had found our group.

The group leader took us to a secret assembly place, in the suburbs of Waldenburg where the rest of the group of refugees was waiting for us so that all of us could leave Poland. We were instructed again not to take more luggage then a person could carry by himself or herself. The reason given was that while we would take the train to the nearest point at the Polish Czech border, from there on we would have to cross the border on foot.

Before leaving Poland all of us were informed that we would be traveling on a Red Cross document listing us as Greek refugees returning home from forced labor camps. None of us was to speak to any border guard. Our leader who was fluent in many languages would be our spokesman.

While none of us spoke Greek we were permitted to speak Hebrew or recite a Hebrew prayer to confuse the border guards. We were also advised to change our dress habits to make us look more Greek. We were told that the Greeks wear their shawls on the outside instead of inside their coats. For head gear many put on berets or old stripped down ladies hats. It was a comedy to look at each other; my brother Paul had on a black ladies hat, and I tore out the brim of my hat to make it look different.

The leader of the group assigned to each of us a New Greek name, which corresponded to the names on his Red Cross document.

We took the train from Waldenburg traveling in the direction of the Czech border. Before we reached the last train stop closest to the Czech border, the Polish conductor locked all the doors to our railroad car. At the next station all the passengers left the train except for our group. We anticipated some trouble. The Polish conductor tried to speak to us in Polish, but all of us pretended that we didn't understand what he was saying and pointed him to our leader. What the conductor requested was for some documentation, since all of us had no identification. Our leader produced the Red Cross papers stating that we were Greek refugees returning home from slave labor camps, and asking all national authorities to help us reach our destination. The document helped, and all of us were released from the train to continue our march to the Czech border. On the way we picked up a guide who was to lead us to our next destination.

We were forewarned that on the Polish side of the border the guards would search us and that we should not make any fuss if they confiscated some of our possessions. It must have been a tacit understanding between the guards and our guide. I had to part with a pair of new shoes; some others lost their watches to the search.

Next we were told to surrender all our Polish currencies since across the border the money would become worthless. After passing his hat and collecting all our Polish Money the soldiers lifted the crossing guardrail and let us walk towards the Czech border, which was only about a hundred yards away.

On the Czech side of the border we had to pass through the same procedure. Again they searched us and confiscated whatever they liked. This time the search was done in a room of the guardhouse.

Next to where my father was standing someone dropped a German banknote. The Czech soldier suspected that my father dropped the money and for that reason detained him. My father was being questioned as to the ownership of the money. True to our instruction my father was reciting a Hebrew prayer with no indication that he understood the questions. The soldier accused him of being a smuggler of German currency and therefore detained him, while the rest of us were let go.

We alerted our guide to what happened and he returned to the guardhouse to intercede on my father's behalf. After another body search my father was released. We boarded the train for our next destination, which was Prague the capital of Czechoslovakia.

The Czech countryside had very few signs of war. The train schedules and train operations were more orderly than in Poland. We arrived in Prague in the late afternoon. We left the railroad station and took a trolley car toward the part of town where the old Jewish museum was located.

After the end of the war the museum served as an assembly point for Jewish refugees crossing the Czech country. At the museum we were registered as refugees and, following registration, were assigned to a nearby displaced persons camp where we were provided with food and lodging. All this was accomplished under the guiding hand of the man from the Bricha organization.

Next morning we went out on the town in the city of Prague. We were astonished with the normalcy in the city. It seemed that there was never a war. After having seen the destruction of Warsaw and other Polish cities, Prague seemed to be picture perfect with no signs of war damage. The coffee houses were open and doing business as usual, the pastry shops were full of baked goodies. People strolling down the boulevard all smiling made us for a moment, forget the horrors of war.

We returned to the Jewish museum in Prague to look for familiar names and faces. The clean walls of the museum served as a bulletin board for survivors of the Holocaust. It was our way of letting other survivors know that we were alive and we are on our way to West Germany. We left our names on the wall of the Jewish museum in Prague as a manifestation of our survival.

On the way from the museum back to the displaced persons camp, my brother Paul and one of his traveling companions were arrested by the Czech Police. The reason for their arrest was that someone overheard them speak Russian and notified the Czech Police who were on the lookout for Russian deserters. We kept our distance from them but were very distressed about their arrest.

As soon as we arrived back into the D.P. camp we called on our leader for help. The leader calmed our fears and advised us that they have a connection with the Czech Police and would see to it that my brother and his companion would be released. After their arrest my brother and his friend were taken down to the main Police station in Prague where they were questioned about their knowledge of Russian. They maintained their innocence and told the Police that they were Greek citizens who were imprisoned by the Germans in Russia and are now returning home. After a few hours, following the intervention of our leader they were released. We were all warned not to speak Russian in public but Yiddish.

We were getting ready to leave the D.P. camp for West Germany. This time we would be traveling as French Jews. Each one of us received a document with a French name stating that we were returning to France from a forced labor camp. I still remember my French name Rechni Cur. Before leaving the D.P. camp we were again reminded not to take more luggage than each one of us could carry. This time the border crossing will be at a mountain trail, which will require more dexterity to carry your own baggage. We were given instructions on the day and time to assemble at the railroad station in Prague to board the train in the direction of the West German border.

While we were getting ready to leave, we received a notice that the camp was being quarantined due to the outbreak of an infectious disease. The entrance to the camp was locked and no one was to leave. All our travel arrangements were already made, so we faced a dilemma. Legally we could not leave the camp for at least three days. This would take us beyond our appointed travel time. Again we fell back on our wartime experience: We cut a hole in the fence surrounding the camp and illegally left the camp. Our next destination was the city of As near Cheb on the Czech and German border.

18

WEST GERMANY D.P. CAMP FOHRENWALD
—SAILING TO AMERICA

The city of As was as close as you can get by train to the German border. Our leader told us that we would cross the border on foot. The crossing would take place at night. The "Bricha"(*Hebrew-escape*) organization had arranged with a guide to smuggle us across to West Germany. To avoid detection by the border guards we had to take a narrow mountain trail.

We marched in single file. In some places the road was covered with snow, which made it very slippery. Among the refugees was a middle-aged woman who took along more baggage than she could carry. In the dark, she slipped on the snow and fell. We stopped to assist her and discovered that she had twisted her ankle. She could hardly walk and had to be helped with her baggage.

My brother and I, the youngest in the group, were assigned to carry her bundles. The extra weight of the bags made me perspire; I felt a chill and soon began to cough. There was no time to stop we had to go on to avoid being captured by the border guards. We managed to elude the Czech guards.

As we crossed to the German side of the border dogs began to bark. Soon after we heard shouts to *"Halt"* Stop. The dogs with their German handlers surrounded us. We were taken to their guardhouse. The guide from the Czech side had disappeared. We were stranded in a no man's land. We had no choice but to level with them. We told them that we were stateless refugees trying to reach West Germany. After a short deliberation, the German Guards allowed all of us to proceed to the nearest railroad station, which was in the town of Selb.

The railroad station was small. All of us squeezed inside to keep warm. The next scheduled train was early on the morning. Our final destination was Munich Germany. The first major stop was the city of Regensburg. We arrived in Munich late in the afternoon. The city still showed the scars of war. The streets were full with skeletons of bombed buildings, including the railroad station. We were informed not to loiter in the streets. We asked for direction to find the *"Deutsche"* German Museum.

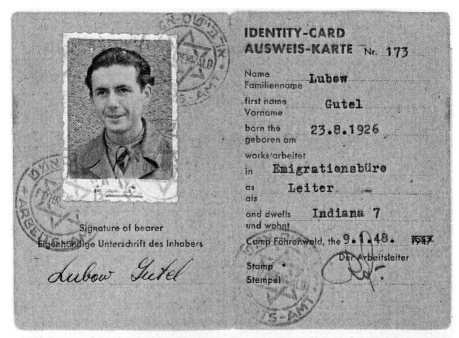

1948:George Identity Card as manager of immigration office D.P. Camp Forenwald West Germany

The museum after the war served as an assembly point for all refugees. After registering with the museum we were provided with food and lodging for the night. Next morning we were provided with transportation to take us to Fohrenwald.

Fohrenwald was organized as a DP *(Displaced Persons)* camp for Jewish survivors of the Holocaust. By the time I arrived into the camp I felt sick. I was running a high fever and was placed in the infirmary. According to the doctor my illness required hospitalization. In the afternoon they transferred me to a major hospital in Munich. The hospital was located in *"Altesheim"* an old age complex, which was spared the destruction of war. The nursing staff was from a religious order. The services the sisters provided were excellent. I entered the hospital with the diagnosis of double pleurisy.

For weeks the fever was high. The doctors prescribed medication to make me sweat. My bed sheets had to be changed constantly to keep me dry. When my temperature dropped to normal I was taken to the X-Ray department. The pictures showed that I had fluid on my lungs, and would require a prolonged stay in the Hospital. The fluid from the lungs was removed with a needle and syringe. Just to look at the big needle would make me sick. For weeks they used the syringe. It was very painful when they had to disengage it from the needle. A resident doctor came up with the idea to seat me up on a high table. The needle was attached to a small rubber tube and the law of physics took over. The fluid drained by itself into a bucket on the floor. This procedure became less painful, and was used until the fluid stopped reappearing.

The hospital stay lasted close to three months. The only visitor I had during all this time was my brother Paul. When he was told not to see me because I was contagious, he used to sneak in by the back entrance and visit me. After three months I was discharged from the hospital and placed in a sanatorium.

The sanatorium was in former Nazi resort place near the town of Garmisch-Partenkirchen. The food and the accommodation were good. Most of the patients were survivors from concentration camps. There were some young ladies from Hungary and we formed a group to play cards. I told them that I was from Poland. My stay in the sanatorium was to last four weeks. My brother Paul used to visit me. His last visit was on a Sunday. The following Wednesday I was to be discharged. On the spur of the moment I decided to leave. I told the management that I was leaving a few days early. Since there was no objection, I left with my brother Paul for Fohrenwald.

My father was glad to see me back in the DP Camp. About the same time we received affidavits from our relatives in the States, we immediately applied for the visas. The American consul in Munich told us that the processing would take a few months. Once all the documents were in order, we would be able to leave for New York.

1947: Photo of reunion of survivors of the Holocaust
From Nowogrodek and surrounding Communities, taken at
D.P. Camp Fohrenwald in West Germany

The first items on the agenda were the health certificates. We all had to pass medical examinations by many doctors. My brother and myself passed all tests. My father was told to undergo minor surgery to pass. After his surgery we submitted all the documents to the council in Munich. After weeks of waiting I inquired with the American council about our visas. The council advised us that there would be a delay.

The reason for the delay was that the United States Congress adopted a law allowing many refugees who were stranded in the States during the war to apply for permanent residency, with one provision that their applications for permanent residence, if accepted, will be charged against the emigration quota of their country of origin. Since many of the refugees were from former Poland, the Polish emigration quota was filled up for the next three years.

It was a terrible disappointment for us; we had no choice but to wait. Life in the DP camp became routine. Paul joined the camp police. The American army provided the training. His job was limited to policing in the camp only. I applied for work and was given a job with the emigration office in the camp.

One day I was asked to come to the police station for an interrogation. I had no idea why they would want to question me. In the police station I met up with the same group of young Hungarian ladies I befriended in the sanatorium. They accused me of being a "Kapo" *(overseer)* in the death camp of Auschwitz. They claimed that I recognized them while we were playing cards, and therefore left the sanatorium early. This episode convinced them that I was the man they were looking for. There must have been someone else in Poland that looked like me. The dates in question were July and August 1944. Lucky for me I had a few friends from my hometown who testified that on that dates I was in Nowogrodek. It was a case of mistaken identity and the ladies apologized.

Camp Fohrenwald held about 3000 inhabitants. Life in the camp was demoralizing. We were provided with all the basic necessities, and were afraid of getting used to life on the dole. This kind of life held no hope for the future. Most were eager to leave Germany. My job in the emigration office was to help applicants with their visa requirements. Countries most eager to accept refugees were Australia and Canada.

Many a DP person registered with more than one country. The majority wanted to go to Palestine in order to start a new life and build a Jewish homeland. The atrocities we suffered during the Nazi occupation of Europe made us want to leave Germany as soon as possible.

American dignitaries visited the DP camp. I remember the visit by the New York Mayor La Guardia. He asked us where do we want to go, in one voice we answered Palestine. There was no future for us in Germany and we were anxiously waiting to leave.

In May 1948 the state of Israel was established. The same year Truman was elected President. He lived up to his pre-election promise that if elected he would allow a 100,000 refugees from the German D.P. Camps to enter the United States disregarding the immigration quotas.

It was the fulfillment of his promise that we finally received our visas. We were notified by the American Consulate in Munich to get ready to leave. After we passed the final medical examination, we were given a time schedule to leave the D.P. camp. Under the guidance of an American official the train took us to the seaport of Bremerhaven.

The trip was interesting; we were already considered American subjects and were provided with all the provisions that an American would be used to, but to us it was a novelty. The dishes on which our food was served were made from paper. We assumed that we had to use them for the entire trip. When the porter informed us that they were disposable we were astonished of this new American luxury.

In Bremerhaven we were told to stay in the assembly location and not to mix with the locals until the day of our departure. While waiting we were briefed by a lady social worker. The lady told us that the ship that will take us to the United Stated was of a better class than the troop carriers. She warned us not to make pigs of ourselves and overeat, since the supply of food would be unlimited.

On a rainy morning we were finally given orders to assemble in the yard of the compound to board buses on a short trip to the ship, which was anchored in Bremerhaven harbor. The name of the ship was S.S.Falcon. Only about three hundred passengers were refugees the balance were American travelers employed by the Government or private industry.

For us the ship was luxurious. We traveled in style with assigned seating arrangements for breakfast, lunch and dinner. Each of the refugees received 6 dollars of spending money from a relief agency. On board there was also a canteen were you could purchase shaving needs, cosmetics and other minor necessities.

The first evening the three of us myself my father and my brother went up to the dining room for our first American dinner. The tables were set for four, the three of us and one other single man made up the foursome. On the table were one set of salt and peppershakers and one big bowl of sugar. While we were used to seeing the small salt and peppershakers the big sugar bowl was a surprise. In our way of thinking we assumed that the sugar was given to us for the entire trip.

Since three of us were from the same family it didn't matter who used more or less sugar, but we felt that the stranger should have his fair share. We emptied out the sugar bowl and divided its contents in four equal amounts. Each one of us received a portion of sugar to last us for the entire trip. The waiter serving our table must have noticed that all the sugar was gone. He took the empty bowl and to our astonishment brought back a full bowl of sugar. All through the war years, sugar was a commodity equal to gold. In the United States it was an inexpensive food staple.

Another surprise to me was the olives, which were placed in a small dish on our table. I had never tasted an olive and from the looks of it I expected a sweet dark cherry. I took one olive and put it in my mouth and after one bite I spit it out. To this day I can't eat olives.

The first day and night on the ship were very peaceful. The North Sea was calm and we enjoyed the trip. Since we were single men our sleeping berths were down in the hull of the ship below the water line. We could hear the water splashing against the sides of the ship. A few of the passengers got seasick and would not leave their berth. So far I felt good and took in the sight from the deck. I spoke in my broken English to the sailors and asked them if this was the way the ship would operate all the way to the States. He laughed and said to wait until we hit the English Channel, we would then feel the difference.

There was a nice looking young lady on board who came from the same DP Camp, Fohrenwald. I was trying to get her attention but could not find the proper moment. The first day and a half passed by leisurely. On the second day in the afternoon we were entering the English Channel. The captain of the ship announced on the loudspeaker that this would be our last chance to see France to the left and England to the right. Once the pilot who guided our ship through the channel disembarked to a small boat, which took him back to Europe, our ship went full speed ahead into the Atlantic Ocean. Some looked with nostalgia to Europe, but to me it was the end of a painful chapter with hope for a new beginning in the promised land of North America.

No sooner did we hit the ocean then our ship started rocking up and down making almost every one seasick. I was on the port side of the ship when I noticed the good-looking girl, turning white; I grabbed her and held her while she was throwing up over the railing. She was very appreciative of my gallantry. I took her down to her berth and immediately rushed back upstairs to the railing to throw up. This was the first and last time I spoke to her. For the next dinner seating we found the dining room almost empty.

One day the weather was very bad. It was raining so heavily, that you could not tell where the sea began and the sky ended. A wall of water was constantly hitting the ship. The foghorn was going full blast, and the ship was rocking up and down like an elevator with your stomach going up and down with each motion. In the daytime I sat in the lounge where the rocking was less troublesome. After midnight I was forced to go down to my berth located in the front of the ship where the rocking was unbearable. My brother Paul was holding up better than I and was able to go down to the dining room and bring my food up to the lounge. After a couple of days I was able to keep my food down. All in all it was a rough voyage.

On the tenth day of our sailing we finally saw land. From afar we could see the skyline of New York and the Statue of Liberty. The ship was not allowed into port because we arrived late in the afternoon. The captain anchored the ship miles from shore and we were told that we would have to wait until the next morning to dock. To entertain us, we were all invited to the captain's dinner. We were served a good meal with all the trimmings. It was a real farewell party with noisemakers, confetti and drinks.

After the party we were allowed to stroll on the deck of the ship. What intrigued me most were objects, which looked from afar not bigger than a matchbox, running up and down the shoreline almost all night? What I discovered later was that we were watching the Belt Parkway in Brooklyn and that the matchboxes were cars.

1954: July 3, Wedding picture of
George and Roslyn.

The next morning the ship was allowed to enter the New York harbor. We docked at a pier in Manhattan. As I was coming down the gangplank of the boat I was looking for familiar faces. Our relatives were notified of our arrival time and there was quite a crowd awaiting our arrival. My father recognized his brothers-in-law and sisters-in-law. When I finally saw my aunt I was shocked, I thought I was seeing a ghost. She was a replica of my grandmother who was killed by the Nazis in December 1941. Although younger in years my aunt looked older than her mother when she was killed. I was introduced to my three cousins one young man and two young ladies. It was then for the first time that I saw and kissed Roslyn. Five years later, after many twists and turns in her life and mine, we were married.

19

NEW YORK

My aunt and uncle greeted us at the pier and took us to their apartment. The apartment was located in Manhattan, in the heart of the garment center at 316 West 36th street. My aunt and uncle, a sister and brother, both in their early forties were unmarried, and shared an apartment. My uncle, a cutter by trade, and my aunt, a seamstress, both worked in the garment industry. My uncle maintained his European piety; each day he attended the morning and evening services in the garment center synagogue next to Macy's department store. Their two-bedroom apartment was ideal for their needs, but it became very congested when the three of us moved in.

After the first two weeks we realized that we would have to move. During the first week we spent our days listening to the radio and to the many Jewish records on the phonograph. My aunt and uncle left every morning to work. For a few days I had difficulty understanding the spoken English. I could read and understand the "Daily News" and was amazed at all the advertisements in the newspaper. After listening to the radio for a week it clicked and I began to understand spoken English.

My father decided to go to visit his boyhood friends who lived all over the city from the Bronx to Brooklyn. One friend was in the wholesale fruit business in the big produce market in the Bronx. He remembered my father from their boyhood in Nowogrodek and were reminiscing of their past. My father was in the same business in Poland but soon realized that New York was not Nowogrodek. Before we parted with his friend we exchanged addresses and telephone numbers. I wrote all the information on a piece of paper and handed it to his friend. His friend gave me a compliment he said, "If I could only write like you". Obviously he was not well educated, yet in America he achieved his dream in the wholesale fruit business.

My brother and I decided that it was time for us to start looking for a job. My aunt Goldie and my uncle Saul did not encourage me to look for a job, instead they told me to go out and look for an empty store and start any kind of business.

Goldie said that if I get a job I would never go into business because once you get a paycheck you would be afraid to lose it. She gave my father the address of another of his boyhood friends who lived in Brooklyn. She told us that he owned a Candy store near Pitkin Ave in Brooklyn.

We visited his friend and spent a whole day with him in his business. The candy store was the kind of business, which my father with his limited English and I could operate. We had to start from scratch. First we had to find a location.

We went looking for a business rental on the lower East side of New York. The lower East side was an area where many Jewish immigrants landed. It still had a large Jewish population. We took the Subway to Essex Street and went looking all over Delancy, Rivington, Stanton and other side streets. On Stanton Street between Pitt and Ridge Street was a boarded up store, which at one time was operated as a candy store. Across the street was a small city park with a swimming pool. We thought that the location was ideal for our needs and went looking for the landlord.

The owners were a Rabbi, who was a principal in a Yeshiva, and his partner a building contractor. They were glad to rent us the store. We paid the first months rent and immediately went to work to restore the place. The building where the store was located was a five story cold flat walk up, which meant it had no elevators or heating. It was built before the turn of the century some time in the middle of the eighteen hundreds. The toilets were in the hallway and were shared by four families. The store had an extra plus, a connecting apartment in the rear. The place now served a double purpose, a place of business and a place to live.

Before we could open the store for business we needed equipment. The main piece of equipment was the fountain. We were told to go to the Bowery where most of the equipment places were located. The price quoted for a stainless steel fountain with cooling coils was more than $3000.00. The amount of money was more than we could afford. We advised the equipment dealer of our predicament. He offered us a solution. His brother in-law was out of a job. He was a furrier by trade, and because of the changes in the fashion industry he was temporarily laid off. If we agreed to take him in as a working Partner we could have the equipment on monthly payments free of any interest charges. Our options were limited and we agreed to the deal.

We formed a partnership with the fictitious name of" Ray's Sweet Shop" and we were on our way to start the business. The equipment dealer was helpful in informing all the companies who would be interested in placing their ice cream in our shop. The ice cream company provided a freezer and compressor including a neon sign to advertise their product.

After all the equipment was installed in the shop, I was advised that since we were selling food products we would have to obtain a license from the Board of Health of the city of New York. We also needed a license from the fire department because the carbonated gas came in a tank under high pressure.

The candy store had a full basement where the compressor and the tank of carbonated gas were kept. I took the subway to the lower part of Manhattan where all the city departments were located. From my experience in dealing with city officials in Poland, Russia and Germany I feared for the worst.

Surprisingly in the United States everything proceeded smoothly. The most helpful was the fire department. I didn't have any knowledge of how to handle the tank of carbonated gas. The fireman gave me a short lecture on how to check the gauge on the tank that controls the pressure of the carbonated gas that flows to the fountain.

I paid the fees for the permit and was on my way out. The fireman was very polite and helpful he took me to the elevator and took me down to the street level to assure that I could find my way out of the city offices. Later I related the story of the fireman to my steady customers who patronized my place. They asked me how much I gave to the fireman for his services. I was very much surprised with their questions. They said it is customary to give a gratuity to the fireman and it's always done in the elevator. I must have been a real disappointment for one of New York's finest.

The police station in our district was a couple of blocks down the street. In the long winter evening I was patronized by many a policemen. I was made aware of an unwritten custom to offer them free coffee and donuts. The security they provided with their presence was appreciated.

In the beginning every day brought a new learning experience how to run the business. From a three cents newspaper to a dime comic book, from two cents plain to a quarter banana split, and from a penny bubble gum to a five cent Hershey bar, all in all a penny business. The summer of 1949 was very hot and the demand for cold drinks was more than expected. We sold two cents plain, five cents coke and the most popular ten cents egg cream. Where the name egg cream came from I don't know. It is a chocolate flavored drink with no cream or egg.

For a dime we sold a scoop of ice cream on a sugary ice cream cone, and for an extra nickel we added an additional scoop. Business was good and in the first year we were able the pay off the balance we owed on the equipment.

When the wintry month came, business slowed down, the demand for cold drinks and ice cream diminished. We were advised by the suppliers to open a lunch counter. All we needed in additional equipment was a steam table, a grill and Silex coffee maker. The counter was able to seat eight people plus eight more on tables in the rear of the store.

We served breakfast, lunch and light dinner. For breakfast the most popular item was a roll with butter and coffee all for fifteen cents. Two eggs any style plus a roll butter and coffee sold for quarter, a deluxe breakfast all of the above plus a fresh squeezed glass of orange juice for thirty-five cents. The restaurant business gave us a pickup for the winter months.

Across the street from the store was the Hamilton Fish recreation park. Many a homeless people hang around the park. One homeless person who had a wooden leg was a daily visitor to buy cigarettes. A pack of cigarettes was twenty cents, but he insisted on buying only two single cigarettes and he offered to pay a few pennies more.

I felt sorry for the man because I thought that he was penniless. Begging was forbidden in the city. The city had a functioning welfare system and the homeless were provided with monies for shelter and food. One of the policemen told me that one day they arrested the one legged man for panhandling. In the wooden leg they found stashed away more than two thousand dollars.

Another interesting customer was an older heavyset gentleman who insisted on drinking his coffee only in a big glass. Coffee was a nickel a cup and each refill was another nickel. I let it slide, because the golden rule of business in America is, the customer is always right.

The man was retired and living on a pension, he kept me company in many an evening. I got to hear his whole life story. He was a traveling salesman, married with a daughter. During the depression he left his family in New York and did not see his daughter for more than twenty years. He traveled all over the country and according to his own story made good money and was able to save some for his old age.

In his old age he became lonely and went looking for his daughter. He found her and tried to reconcile with her, he showered her with gifts but at the end she rejected him. He could not understand why. She told him that when she needed a father he was not around. Her argument was valid but he could not understand it.

I learned in the candy store business and later in the dress business that besides providing a service you also have to listen to customer's problems and smile. Once the candy store became a Luncheonette I had to obtain a restaurant License from the health departments in the city of New York. Soon after a health inspector checked out the premises and issued a violation. He spotted paper napkins under the fountain and he told me that the toilet facilities needed cleaning and repairs. He gave me four weeks to clean up the place. The inside of the store was no problem, but the toilet in the hallway required expensive repairs.

I related the problem to one of my customers. The customer advised me that a twenty-dollar bill could solve the whole problem. He told me that next time when the inspector does his inspection, he would surely take you into the bathroom the check the toilet. It is then that you take out a twenty-dollar bill from your shirt pocket and hand to the inspector. The trick worked and the violations were removed.

Years later I read an article in the Daily News about an investigation in the health department. They discovered that the inspectors who were earning only about ten thousand dollars a year, were living in one hundred thousand dollars mansions, enough said.

A group of customers regularly showed up for breakfast around 11 A.M. They were neatly dressed, ordered a deluxe breakfast consisting of freshly squeezed orange juice, scrambled eggs, roll and butter and coffee. They treated me with respect and were good tippers. Later on, I was told by one of my customers that they were members of the mafia. He assured me that I had nothing to fear, because the place they patronize is safe.

These were just a few of interesting customers who patronized my candy store and luncheonette business.

The candy store was a good place to learn the American way of business. My customers represented a miniature replica of American life. Television was becoming as popular a medium as the Radio. I was always interested in electronics. A friend of my aunt Goldie was part owner of the Eastern school of Radio and Television. He offered me the opportunity to attend the school tuition free.

Most of students were former GI's who attended the school under the GI bill of rights. I graduated as a television repair mechanic. I ordered business cards and handed them out to my candy store customers. The television repair business became my sideline. I also took a couple of semesters in economics, accounting and political science in Brooklyn College.

In the political science class I often expressed my view on the "workers paradise" in the Soviet Union. Many students could not accept the truth. I was accused of being an agent of the FBI, and spreading anti-Soviet propaganda. I'm glad to say that time has proven me right.

20

CALIFORNIA

I arrived in the USA March 29, 1949 with three dollars in my pocket. After a few weeks my father and I went into business. As I described before, we opened a candy store on the lower east side at 127 Stanton St, between Ridge and Pitt Streets. The business offered us a chance to get back on our feet and not to be dependent on anyone. The hours were long since the store was open 6 days a week from 6 in the morning until 12 midnights. In 1952 ten years after the Nazis killed my mother my father remarried. The woman he married was a widow from our hometown in Poland. Her husband had died the first year after they arrived in the USA. A cousin of hers was the matchmaker. My father's second wife had two sons about the same ages as my brother Paul and I. They were both married. One lived in New York and the other one in Chicago. My stepmother was anxious for Paul and I to get married. Paul was introduced to Betty and after a short courtship they were married in October 1953. I dated a few girls, but fell in love with my cousin Roslyn, and in July 1954 we were married.

In New York, life for new Americans was not easy. One of my stepbrothers Benjamin left for California to join his uncle in business. His Uncle Norman Shulman owned the CAROLINE'S Dress shop in Monrovia. He urged us to come to California to start a new life. My brother Paul was the first of us to pioneer out west. Being an electrician it was easier for him to get established. My brother and stepbrother urged me to come west. I took their advice and on February 18th, 1956 I left New York for California.

I took the train to Chicago where I met my stepbrother Bill. He took me to his house to meet his family. Sarah, Bill's wife and Tonia, Benjamin wife were childhood friends of mine as far back as my kindergarten years. I rested a couple of hours in Chicago and then took the train to California. The train stopped in Pasadena, Paul and Betty were there to greet me and take me to their apartment in Monrovia. My stepbrother's Uncle Norman Shulman offered me a job in Caroline's Dress Shop in Monrovia, so that I could learn the dress business. Roslyn was still in New York, and in April 1956 came out by plane to visit me. We both decided that California was the place for us. She went back to New York packed up all our belongings and had them shipped to California. She took the train with some luggage and arrived in Pasadena where my brother Paul and I awaited her. We rented an apartment in Monrovia and settled down to a new life in California. In November 1957, after our first daughter Bonnie was born, I opened my first Dress Shop in South Pasadena under the name of Caroline's Jr. In August 1959 after our second daughter Elana was born, I opened my second dress shop In Montrose. Our third daughter Zvia was born in 1961.

In 1957 I joined Temple Beth Israel in Sierra Madre and in 1959 we bought our first house in Monrovia. In 1964 after the Sierra Madre and the El Monte Synagogue joined together to form the Foothill Jewish Temple and Center, we moved to Arcadia. The name was later changed To Congregation Shaarei Tikvah. When my children started religious school, I became a member of the education committee of the Congregation. For many years I was chairman of the education committee in Shaarei Tikvah. I joined the Men's club in 1957 and in 1967/68 was elected Club President and again in 1986/87. For more than a decade I was treasurer of the Men's Club. I'm an active member of the Men's Club to this

My three daughters, from left to right, Bonnie, Zvia, Elana.

day. For many years I was Vice President for ritual in Congregation Shaarei Tikvah. I was also involved with the Los Angeles Jewish Federation in the Eastern Area and in 1968, 1969 and 1970 I was chairman for the north San Gabriel Valley, United Jewish Welfare Fund Drive. I'm a member of the David Goldman Bnai B'rith Lodge, and also served as president of the San Gabriel Lodge. In general California has been good to me. I was able to raise three beautiful daughters. I made sure that they all got a college education.

My own experience taught me that knowledge is the most precious possession.

In 1994 after 37 years in the same business and at the same location I
retired. My greatest pleasures in life now, are my wife, my children and grandchildren, with their families and friends. My oldest and most reliable friend is
my brother Paul and his family.

As a Jew, the synagogue is the place for prayer, study and assembly and also
the source of my strength.

Having suffered so much in my youth, and having lost 10 formative years
of my life in wars, ghetto, forced labor camp, hiding out in an underground
bunker, army and D.P. Camp, I'm thankful to God for giving me the ability
and strength to overcome adversity and the ups and downs of life.

HOLOCAUST MONUMENT in the forest of
  Skridleve near Nowogrodek
In this mass grave are buried 5100 Jews,
Men, women and children killed by the Nazis
And their helpers on December 8,1941.The
Grandmother of Paul, George and Osher, four
Uncles, six aunts and more than twenty cousins
Were among the victims.

IN MEMORY OF
THE OSTASZYNSKI FAMILY

Grandfather   Pejsach Ostaszynski married to

Grandmother   Esther Chana Leibowicz

They had 6 children all married and all living in Nowogrodek
Following are their names and date of birth:

Peshke	*ChaimVelvl-*	Leike-	Moshe-	*Beines-*	Avremel-
1892	1894	1898	1900	1904	1906

Married to:

Avremel	Cipke	Faivel	Sore-Yente	Beilke	Sara-Malke
Abramowicz	Abramowicz	Kancewik	Polonski	Lubczanski	Shabakowski
Children:				(now **Lubow**)	
Yehoshua	*Daniel*	Osher	Esther	*Pejsach*	Esther
Pejsach	Esther	Nachman	Perle	*Gutel*	Broche
Esther	*Perle*	Luba	Asne	Osher	Mere
	Itzie	Mendel	Pejsach		Pejsach
	Pejsach				
	Batia Rivke				

The 8 underlined names survived the Holocaust

6 Aunts, 4Uncles, and 18 cousins a total of 28 family members were killed, victims of the Holocaust.

To honor the memory of my mother we adopted the <u>Lubow</u> family name.

HOLOCAUST MONUMENT in Litovke
       Near Nowogrodek
In this mass grave are buried more than
5500 Jews men, women and children from
The city of Nowogrodek and the surrounding
Communities, victims of the second and
 Third mass murder of Jews by the Nazis
And their helpers. August 8,1942,February
4,1943.Beilke the mother of Paul, George
And Osher was among the victims

HOLOCAUST MONUMENT in Horodilevke,
Near Nowogrodek
In this mass grave are buried 250 Jews,
Men and women from the Labor Camp
Nowogrodek, killed by the Nazis and the
Local police on May 7,1943. Osher the younger
Brother of Paul and George Lubow was among
The victims.

EPILOGUE

Since NBC televised the "Holocaust," people from every walk of life, often ask me the same question. "Why didn't we resist?" I will answer the question with my own questions.

Where were they then, so brave now in the comfort of their soft chairs watching television? Where was the volunteer brigade who rushed to save those caught in the uprising in the Ghetto of Warsaw?

Tell me the date and the place an attempt was made to parachute in arms, men and medical supplies? Where were all the demonstrators who chained themselves to the White House fence, requesting justice and to warn of the murderers? Tell me the date and the time and the place any of you old enough, marched in protest?

Yes, we did not fight back. We had no standing army, no armaments, no stockpiles of ammunition and no factories to produce them. And let's assume, by some miracle, we became armed. Who would have expected a handful of Jews in Poland to defeat the German army? The same army which in a "blitz-krieg" in 14 days defeated Poland, in 17 days defeated France, in less than three months almost drowned the English at Dunkirk and on the Eastern Front stood at the gates of Moscow? The same army, which in defeat, fought the entire Soviet and Allied forces in Europe for almost one year.

The question should not be directed to the victims, but to the killers and the entire German nation. Why did they kill? Why did they torture? Why did doctors and lawyers become mass killers? Why did the civilized world keep quiet when thousands upon thousands were gassed daily?

The silent looks from our brother and sisters, the compassion of our dead mothers and fathers, begs us to ask the question?

And we the survivors, and believers in humanity, should demand an accounting from all civilized people of the world. We survivors had no influence, no power, but were ready to sacrifice everything to save a child.

It is difficult to describe hunger unless you have been hungry yourself.

It is even more difficult to describe our pain unless you were there.

I hope that by remembering the past, future generations will avoid the pain and suffering of my era.

Having suffered so much in my youth, and having lost 10 formative years of my life in wars, ghetto, forced labor camp, hiding in an underground bunker, army and DP camp. I am thankful to God for giving me the strength and ability to overcome adversity.

My philosophy on life is "do it and God will help you", but don't expect God to do all the work. We must start the action and with the help of God we will succeed.

About the Author

George Lubow was born in the small town of Nowogrodek; in what was once Eastern Poland, now Byelorussia. I am a retired businessman and Holocaust survivor. I felt obligated to write this book so future generations would know and remember the horrors experienced during World War II. The generation of survivors is passing on. We must also remember that in the darkest hour there were Righteous Gentiles who risked their lives to save us.

Please note: Polish spelling is some times used in the names of cities and families.

0-595-32973-X

Printed in the United States
24441LVS00006B/251

9 780595 329731